LABOR'S CIVIL WAR

LABOR'S
CIVIL WAR

BY

HERBERT HARRIS

GREENWOOD PRESS, PUBLISHERS
NEW YORK

Copyright © 1940 by Alfred A. Knopf

First Greenwood Reprinting 1969

Library of Congress Catalogue Card Number 78-90522

SBN 8371-2285-6

PRINTED IN UNITED STATES OF AMERICA

TO

MY FATHER

A MAN OF PEACE

CONTENTS

LABOR'S CIVIL WAR

CHAPTER I

IS LABOR DIGGING ITS OWN GRAVE?

THE AMERICAN labor movement today is numerically stronger than ever before, yet it has entered the crucial decade of the 1940's in a position of great and growing weakness. To be sure, under the auspices of the New Deal, union membership in the United States mushroomed up from a scant three million in 1933 to nearly nine million [1] at the present time. And certainly this gain, whether measured against population or the nation's employed or in any other fashion, remains in both absolute and relative terms the greatest ever recorded by organized labor not only in seven years but in seventeen or seventy.

[1] Out of a potential twenty-five million men, women, and children who colloquially are called the "working class."

Yet the reality beneath this appearance of vast new power does not bear out the promise of union labor's statistical advance. Primarily as a result of the AFL-CIO cleavage, Manhattan cutter and Montgomery lint-head, Boston shoe-worker and Blue Mountain lumberjack alike run the risk that their new lifeline of social and economic rights will become a rope of sand; that their modern Magna Carta, the Wagner Act, will be amended into nullity; that their political potency will be castrated into a prurient eunuchdom; that their ability to strike, to boycott, to picket, will continue to be curtailed as in Oregon, Wisconsin, Pennsylvania, and many other states; that the internal affairs of unions will be more and more regulated by a national government responding to the pressure of a public opinion rendered increasingly hostile by the repercussions of the AFL-CIO feud.

The contention by various labor spokesmen that "it isn't going to be that bad" would seem to be mainly wishful thinking with overtones of inertia—especially at a time when this country is bending its energies toward carrying out a preparedness program that almost hourly assumes a greater sweep, a more martial momentum. Nor will the old saw that unionism in American annals has moved ahead, retreated, but emerged always bigger and better, over any given period, suffice any longer. When Samuel Gompers shortly before his death voiced this view, events were already

4

proving its falsity. In these days of crisis, when the tempo of transition from past to present, from old forms to new, has been immensely speeded up, this whole doctrine of "Take it easy, hope for the best, history shows that we have setbacks, but always recover and go ahead," is fit only for addicts of marihuana or for the kind of "realistic, practical" labor people who, by refusing to face the facts, could teach Don Quixote's ghost the alpha and omega of windmill romanticism.

At the moment, unionism—both as a folk movement and as a form of economic organization—is our first line of defense against an American variant of the totalitarian idea. After all, it was on April 15, 1926 that Il Duce signed the "Legal Discipline of Collective Labor Relations," first item on the legislative agenda of the Fascist state.

It was a year to a day after Der Führer seized the substance and symbols of state power that the up-and-coming Dr. Robert Ley reported the "full and unhampered" operation of the Nazi Labor Front.

In Russia the 170 unions which compose the labor pyramid rise vertically from committee to council into the hands of Joseph Stalin. Indeed, in 1931 it was he who personally laid down the famous Six Points [1]—en-

---

[1] "We can no longer have the situation," Stalin then declared, "where an iron-founder is paid the same as a cleaner, and an engine-driver no more than a copyist." He also insisted that unions must fight against "lack of responsibility," especially toward the care and in-

forced by the GPU—as a guide to union behavior.
Automatically dictatorships deprive workers of freedom of speech and action, of the chance to arrive at
decisions, good, bad, or indifferent, by means of discussion and debate among themselves. In Italy and
Germany, as in Russia, anyone who "calls" a strike is
exiled, imprisoned, or shot. In all three countries the
arbitration courts which in theory are designed to adjust differences between workers and "management"
settle nothing except the hash of dissidents.

It is a point too often neglected that complete control over the producing force is the keystone of the
totalitarian state, which in this respect merely repeats
the tyranny of Pharaohs and Caesars over their slaves,
of margraves and barons over their serfs, of English
entrepreneurs over their mine and mill workers when
the Industrial Revolution was young.

The need to preserve and enlarge the scope of a free
and independent unionism in the United States is therefore not alone labor's problem. It cannot be divorced
from the larger issue of making American democracy
work—in the sense of attaining to a tolerably just society where the individual's opportunity for self-de-
velopment, materially and spiritually, will become if
not equal (it never was or can be that, save as a meta-

stallation of machinery; must overcome their "petit-bourgeois"
prejudices about equalizing all wages and their suspicion of "specialists"; must master modern "technics" in production and use genuine "cost-accounting" methods.

6

physical abstraction) at least infinitely more pervasive than it is; at least available to millions who now find the very phrase "equality of opportunity" a hollow and pretentious parody of the promise of American life.

Whether you approve of unions or wish them in Halifax, they undeniably in this regard perform services which—far less spectacular than strikes—are far more important to the national well-being. In the first place, they are the great stabilizers of the American economic system. Like the gyroscopes on big modern ocean liners, they aid in steering a steadier, smoother course. Our society is after all geared on a mass-production basis. And to sell the goods—whether clothes or cars or candy—released by mass production we need mass purchasing power, which is impossible to achieve on any solid ground unless sufficient dollars are pumped down into the lower brackets where the velocity of exchanging money for goods remains always very constant and very high.

It is at this point that unions, in seeking to obtain fair and better pay for their members, assist the rest of the national community in preserving and increasing their own incomes. In bad times, unions try, often successfully, to maintain wage and salary levels against the downward pull of what, without them, could more readily turn into a runaway deflation, that prelude to panic and near collapse. In good times, unions try to put wages and salaries up still higher, helping to even

7

the balance between the production and marketing of commodities. And whether by contract with the separate concern within an industry, or with a trade association covering part or the whole of that industry, unions provide that predictable in labor costs without which stable prices are only a monetary mirage. It is by such methods that unions protect and extend the ability to buy not only for their own adherents but for countless others as well. Nor should it be forgotten, amid the stress and excitement of the current emergency, that the operation of this principle is even more important for preserving the functional equilibrium, and for bracing the national morale of a semi-war, or even a full war, economy as for a peace-time economy.

There are about nine million unionists in the United States today, 1,090,052 [1] of whom, incidentally were involved in strike activity of one kind or another during 1939. Together with their families (the statistical family is estimated at 4.1 members) they comprise about twenty-five per cent of the total population. They buy a vast quantity of bread and furniture and electric light and they pay a lot of rent.

Whenever a union is weakened at a particular plant or blotted out entirely, pay-envelopes begin to shrink, and shrink again, with alarming rapidity, as statistics

---

[1] This includes the 343,500 workers affected by the bituminous coal stoppage during April and May 1939, an occurrence which has been variously described as a lock-out, a suspension, and a strike.

and experience abundantly prove. When therefore an organization like the Associated Farmers—the supporters of which plow the fields and gather the harvests from sumptuous board of directors' rooms in San Francisco banks and Seattle skyscrapers—attempts to extend its "Curb the unions" campaign, state by state, from the west coast to the Atlantic seaboard, it is not only aiming to drive labor's wage into the depths of our new pauperism. It is also pulling the props from under whatever economic stability we may have left at this time; to prepare the red ink for many a ledger, to bring discharge slips to many a non-union American, and in general to debase national living standards.

In the long run, of course, any employer who fights the growth and functioning of a bona-fide unionism, either in his own company or elsewhere, is a saboteur of American business enterprise. He is far more subversive than any Red. He is—perhaps unconsciously—doing his best to hasten the day when we too will have forced labor unstead of a labor force, and when—as in the Third Reich, or under Mussolini—he may retain the legal title to his property, but be compelled to act as the "servant" of an omnicompetent state carrying out the orders of a one-party bureaucracy.[1]

[1] In this connection it is interesting to observe that in Russia the genus businessman was abolished at first, then restored under the NEP, then exterminated completely. In Germany, and to a lesser extent in Italy, there has been an oblique crustacean-like advance toward this same goal. Under the Nazi regime, for example, even

9

If the current union-busting campaign—as carried on by certain employing interests on the one hand and by alleged labor statesmen on the other—attains the great success it seems headed for, the consequences will be appalling. To begin with, the decline of unionism in normal times curtails purchasing power, contributes overwhelmingly to economic stagnation; this in turn induces more unemployment and further sterilizes any new capital investment. In the present abnormal situation, it would also widen the gap between labor's income and its living costs, even if the resulting slack in capital investment were temporarily taken up by the government in the form perhaps of new armaments appropriations. And yet the results of this whole process in either case cannot be assessed in financial terms alone.

A man joins a union to improve his income, true enough. But that is not his only motive. He joins to avoid being pushed around, to assert his own dignity as an inhabitant of the United States, and to enjoy a sense of fraternity with others like him, even if it's only playing poker with the boys at the union hall. As an American he has inherited a tradition of independence

---

before the second World War, the manufacturer was not permitted to bargain on the costs of his raw materials, or to determine his selling price, or to import or export as he might have desired, or merge with a competitor, or invest surplus funds unless any and all of these actions promoted the "common good" as defined and ordained by the Hitler hierarchy.

10

and, however threadbare it may be in practice, it is still alluring to him as ideal; and it is something that he as a rule can move toward only by acting within the framework of his own group. Otherwise he has virtually neither voice nor vote in the conduct of his job.

When his union is destroyed, or when he is stopped from forming one by, for instance, the Ford Motor Company's technique of maiming or merely "mussing up" would-be unionists, he feels cheated of his due. He has been denied a vehicle of both economic and emotional self-expression, the latter amply attested by the interminable soundings-off at the usual union meeting. He has the sensation of being stepped on, of being humiliated, of being not quite a man—attitudes which frequently inspire the retaliation of spontaneous flare-ups in the factory, and of that ca' canny (soldiering on the job) which drives straw-bosses to drink. And what is more important, the worker deprived of his chance to say anything effective about the conditions of his employment is reduced to the psychological status of those others who are compelled to take what is handed out, whether a dole or a semi-starvation wage, and no back talk about it either.

Under such circumstances, intensified by the depression's high scarcity of jobs, which for most workers has made a change to other employment a wholly academic question, he tends to develop a profound resent-

11

ment not only against management but also against his environment. And it is this feeling of grievance, of not counting, that is still turning an ever larger number of the unorganized into the dupes of demagogy, crackpot, racist, shirted and hooded. In any such atmosphere of frustration neither patriotism nor faith in democracy can be said to thrive.

The non-union employee, on the whole, knows even less about the facts of life, economically, than the unionist. The latter at least acquires some glimmering of what it's all about, of what matters to him as a worker, if only from the report of the delegate to the national convention or editorials and reprints in the union paper. But the non-affiliated worker lacks this knowledge, meagre and rudimentary as it too often is. Hence in the North, in Michigan and Ohio, for example, he is especially susceptible to the intense chauvinism and secret ceremonial flummery of the Bullet Club and similar successors to the Black Legion. Below Mason and Dixon's line he is the doubly deluded rank and filer in a rapidly reviving Ku Klux Klan pledged to extirpate unionism in the South.

Moreover, the hazard of undermining or thwarting unionism appears especially acute when considered against the background of our own native trends toward an incipient Fascism. They are more dangerous by far than Fifth Columns and Trojan Horses planted and cultivated here by foreign governments, and are

12

as likely to be accentuated as arrested by preparation for war.

We still have some ten million [1] unemployed who, with their dependents, comprise twenty-three per cent of our total population existing outside the rim of the "normal" economic circle. They don't "belong," they are the new untouchables. Too often they are treated with contempt, and ridiculed as lazy or incompetent, as lacking the wit and gumption for making the grade. They are oppressed, even on WPA, by that intensely American sense of guilt and failure afflicting those unable to keep within the orbit of earning their livelihoods in the accepted fashion. By the hundreds of thousands they have undergone the anguish of a poverty bordering on starvation. They are also anxious to regain lost "face." They want work and security; and they are reaching the point where they are ready to exchange personal freedom for the assurance of eating regularly, of being employed at something that will restore their faith in themselves. To more and more of

[1] At the present rate of armament expenditures, a maximum of 1,500,000 workers, chiefly in the skilled occupations required in aircraft, machine-tool, shipbuilding and other primary war industries, can be absorbed during the year from July 1940 to July 1941. Another 1,000,000 youth to be instructed by the government in noncombat services, for a year, or to be given special vocational training, may also be taken out of the ranks of the "idle." Military recruiting is expected to absorb 300,000 more during the next twelve months. Yet all this leaves a backlog of around 7,000,000 unemployed who, because of the spotty and spurious nature of a war-based "prosperity," may be with us for years, unless war actually comes, and even then many of them may not be "needed."

13

them the very concept of liberty is a luxury of the well fed. At the same time, since nobody likes to blame himself for his misfortunes, and since they as a rule know next to nothing of basic cause-and-effect relationships within their economy, they often seize the nearest whipping-boy on which to vent their dissatisfactions. Their plight then becomes not the "fault" of a complex interplay of social forces, but the fault of the Jews, or the international bankers, or the politicians, or the aliens, or Wall Street, or the Catholic Church, or whatever simple scapegoat may be made to serve their inner need for absolution.

We have, in addition, more than six million youth who have come of working age since 1929, some two thirds of them without employment. Various surveys, conducted by *Fortune* and the Y.M.C.A. and other agencies, show anywhere from twenty to forty per cent of them immensely discouraged and even embittered, sure that only pull or influence will give them a crack at any kind of job, a chance to marry, to build a home, while almost every advertisement they read and every movie they attend present tantalizing images of the kinds of things they want but cannot obtain, even in small degree.

We are repeating in our present persecution of minority groups the anti-alien errors of the Know-Nothing movement of the 1850's, the Mitchell Palmer raids

14

in 1920 upon "radicals," only now on a bigger scale.[1] We have Father Coughlin suggesting, and General Moseley openly advocating, the efficacy of pogroms as the way out of our present difficulties. We have, besides, a clamorous conformity in thought and opinion, an intolerance exemplified among the "best people" by the rite-minded Bishop Manning and, among others lower down on the social scale, by his street-corner alter ego, "Big-Mouth Joe" McWilliams of the Christian Front. Despite war booms and boomlets, we are subjected to a vast new barrage of monetary schemes for our quick salvation. The Townsend Plan, which in sheer vacuity and fuzziness exceeds the most fantastic panaceas offered by Black and Brown orators, is merely the best known of twenty others which, by offering a single sure solution for all our ailments, merely intensify the quest for a simple cure-all.

We have 3,000,000 tenant farmers, and 50,000 acreage-owning farmers, losing their land, their homes, their livestock, every year. We have at our lowest-income extreme 2,900,000 non-relief families who receive less than $340 a year; and at the highest extreme 290,000 families who get $10,000 or more annually. In the intermediate groups we have 87 per cent of our families getting along on less than $2,500 a year, and 42 per cent of these on less than $1,000.

[1] There are 3,598,000 voteless aliens in the United States today.

We have millions of the precariously solvent among the lower and median middle classes who more and more resent the necessity of supporting the indigent by taxes or by charity to relatives. Many, particularly in this social stratum, survived the depression's first years only by drawing out savings and borrowing on life-insurance policies and in the current "recession" have nothing left to fall back on except their naked courage—when courage is not enough.

We have our little businessman—small manufacturer, wholesaler, storekeeper—feeling caught between the Scylla and Charybdis of demands for increased wages on the part of unions, and a ruthless rivalry on the part of Big Ownership as the fight for an ever larger share of the consumer's dwindling dollar attains a new ferocity. And we have a concentration of control over finance and industry that places the policy direction of fifty per cent of our entire producing and monetary apparatus in the hands of less than two thousand individuals, most of whom invoke the laissez-faire precepts of Adam Smith at the very moment they are profiting from their own private collectivisms of the holding company, their own planned economies of monopolistic competition.

We have, moreover, a widespread and vexing recognition that "something is wrong," that it's irrational to allow destitution to exist side by side with the most magnificent machinery for turning out the necessaries and comforts of living that has ever been built in the annals of mankind. We have a Communist Party which, despite its inability to poll more than one per cent of the national vote, can be blown up into a bogy man at will and whim, at the same time that it gives the kiss of death to any cause—no matter how otherwise admirable—with which it manages to identify itself. Our press, both daily and weekly, is on the whole so ultra-conservative, so tender of the prejudices of advertisers, that it constantly indulges in infantile tantrums over the mildest reforms, finding in them the threat of a non-existent revolution from the Left, whipping up around them imaginary perils to that semantic monstrosity, "Americanism," and neglecting to heed the one valid and prophetic legacy of Huey Long: namely, that "When Fascism comes to America, it will be in the name of Anti-Fascism," that when the strong man rides among us his horse will be caparisoned in the Stars and Stripes.

We are developing in city slums, with their rising rowdyism and criminality, and in the ditch-bank camps of Okie and Arkie, with their mounting protests that "Anything could be better than this," a new American *Lumpenproleterit*, without moorings, first portent of a society that has begun to rot at its roots.

We have as a people a deep hatred of Nazism, Fascism, Communism; but their most eloquent foes in Democratic and Republican ranks have so far shown no capacity for evolving a program to eradicate the underlying dislocations and discontents which give rise to the totalitarian state. The New Deal wing of the Democrats has been conscious that this problem exists: and even dramatized the questions which it raises. But the New Deal answers, by and large, have been too superficial to be effective, while the dominating group within the G.O.P. denies that the problem, as a need to adapt ourselves to the dynamics of a new day, really exists.

And as we as a nation continue our mean-whiling with makeshifts, we are getting ourselves all confused by an orgy of name-calling in which the simple demand for a better wage is painted as red and good old-fashioned American conservatism is painted brown or black, and the search for a way out premised upon the national interest is submerged in a contest between social groups more sharply defined and more mutually distrustful and angry than at any time since the Civil War, although national unity is the need of the hour.

If to these and many similar chemicals already fuming in the crucible of a potential dictatorship we add, as a final ingredient, the destruction of the labor movement, with its instinctive checks upon absolutism, we may well find this to be the catalytic agent that makes the reaction go to an end—the end of the democratic process.

Our vaunted 175,000 separate and distinct units of

18

government, our hundred and fifty years of practice in approximating a political democracy, our tradition of civil liberties, may not then be safeguards potent enough to fend off the march of the new barbarism; to remedy soon enough the vast increase in the jobless and in personal frustration that a breakdown in the moral and economic bulwarks of unionism will inevitably precipitate; and to relieve the agonizing sense of insecurity and fear for the future on which the "leadership principle" thrives, if only because its practitioners promise to bring order, meaning, and certainty into a baffling life.

Whether the future holds peace or war, it would seem the supreme obligation of the labor movement to take the initiative in seeking to remove the institutional lags and maladjustments which prevent the smoother and more just and efficient functioning of our power-age society. In fact, the labor movement is in the position of the man who, to save his own house from burning, has to put out fires next door and across the street. Yet in the face of an exigent need for a unified, constructive unionism, aware that its own well-being is inseparable from that of all other elements in the population, there are divided councils and mutually destructive strife.

Within recent history there have been two tragic and pertinent parallels to this situation. For five years, beginning in 1919, the split in the Italian Confederation of Labor between Socialist and strictly trade-union elements preceded and in large measure provoked the March on Rome. From the mid twenties forward, the bitter relentless warfare between the Social-Democratic and Communist unionists in Germany was not only the simple and deadly dagger placed at the heart of the Weimar Republic but also—more than any other single immediate factor—prepared the way for Hitler's assumption of the Chancellorship in 1933. In the United States today, both AFL and CIO are weakening each other and bringing down upon their heads the wrath and suspicion of the public and their own memberships, quite as if the totalitarian menace did not exist; as if the experiences of the Italian and German labor movements were examples to be emulated, rather than shunned.

It is a crowning irony that the attacks against unionism, both frontal assault and mining and sapping of the walls, come less effectively from the expected opposition than from the ranks of labor itself. The fight between the AFL and the CIO is quickly moving toward a double suicide of majestic stupidity and not only because of quarrels on the plane of jurisdiction. During the past eight years as the federal government, not as a plot of the New Dealers, but in response to urgent necessity, has encroached increasingly upon every phase of the national scene, the contest for the union's right to be, to become, to endure, has been in large part shifted from mine tipple and factory gate to the ballot-box. Labor's political strength has become as important as its economic power, its influence with legislators as important as its influence with employers. Hence, to protect such legislative gains as the National Labor Relations Act, the labor movement has to participate in the political arena with more vigor and intelligence and cogency than it has previously displayed. The constant pressure by reactionary interests to use the national defense program as an excuse for "relaxing labor laws," while profits attain new dazzling heights, is an omen that unionism's darkest days may lie just ahead. Yet so long as its political efficacy is suborned by the AFL-CIO feud, it will continue to be kicked around, as it now is, with impunity and contempt. And unless the AFL-CIO breach is healed the government benisons which from 1933 to 1938 were considered as paradise enow will keep turning into boomerangs from 1940 forward.

CHAPTER II

SCHISM IN LABOR'S CHURCH

AT ITS 1931 convention in Vancouver, the American Federation of Labor commemorated the fiftieth anniversary of its founding. But this affair was keyed more to the somber tones of a funeral dirge than to the crashing cymbals of jubilee. The Federation was in a bad way. Its influence was waning. Dues-paying members were dropping out at the rate of seven thousand a week as layoffs became epidemic. Editors and economists, columnists and commentators were wondering out loud whether or not labor unions in this country could survive the rigors of what was already being recognized as a new and different kind of depression. In industry after industry AFL wage-scales and hour-schedules, built up through years of struggle and sacrifice, were being discarded at a moment's notice. The labor market was glutted with seven million unemployed, daily growing more numerous and desperate, eager to grab any kind of work on any terms, undermining union standards from coast to coast.

Looking backward to escape the present's perplexity and the future's qualms, orators of the occasion sought to recapture the grandeur of the Federation's past, crediting the AFL with almost every advance in American labor's status. Yet such was their own mood of pessimism, and their need to make bricks without straw, that they stressed the adoption of the Australian ballot, free text-books in the schools, the direct election of senators, and the establishment of five puny unions in Puerto Rico as instances of "labor's magnificent progress."

Speaker after speaker affirmed that nearly all the AFL's accomplishments—economic, educational, ethical—stemmed from its devotion to the principle of "voluntarism" fashioned by the Federation's patron saint, Samuel Gompers.

"Voluntarism," of course, is to labor what *laissez faire* is to business. Under this credo, workers—when mobilized into unions of of their own free choice—were to rely upon their economic strength alone, their ability jointly to withdraw their skill and labor-energy. They were to refrain from invoking government assistance lest they become "wards of the state." Of course, in the same way that a manufacturer might ask Congress to

23

raise the tariff on his particular article and thus protect him against foreign competition, the AFL might ask Congress to restrict foreign immigration, to protect AFL members from foreign competition for their jobs. But over and above this essentially negative kind of legislation, the Federation wanted the government to keep its hands off, believing the less it "interfered" with labor affairs the better. Yet all the rhetorical tributes paid to the virtues of voluntarism at the 1931 meeting failed to dispel the gloom that permeated every gathering of delegates like Pittsburgh smog.

Two years later, however, this despair became rejoicing. In October 1933 the AFL's annual convention in Washington, D. C., this time coincided with the unveiling of the Gompers memorial. The Federation was on the crest of the wave. Its leaders were revitalized, its morale restored. Recruits to unionism were thronging before the Federation's gates as rapidly as the AFL had lost them two years before.

In this interval, AFL leaders—bewildered by the percussions of the panic and by the bankruptcy of "voluntarism"—had turned, like their business prototypes, to the national government in Washington to rescue them from the consequences of their own myopia.

On June 16, 1933 Section 7a of the National Industrial Recovery Act had given to the AFL and to other American workers something they had always had on paper but had never possessed in actuality: the un-

24

hampered right to bargain collectively through unions of their own choosing—a right that, it was promised, was going to be enforced by the ultimate powers of the federal government itself.

At this point the high gods of irony must have rocked with laughter. The new courage and confidence displayed by delegates to the Gompers ceremony derived from a complete repudiation of the philosophy which he had developed as the Federation's lodestar and foundation stone. The distrust of government intervention which had been an AFL byword since its inception in 1881 had been replaced by acceptance of government aid to unionization on a more-the-merrier basis.

William Green, president of the AFL, in the same speech found room to be eloquent about Gompers's great role in guiding the Federation, and to hail Section 7a as labor's "new Magna Carta," the Blue Eagle's most resplendent feather.

He and other AFL chieftains were convinced that, at long last, 7a empowered them to overcome the stubborn resistance of American employers to unionism—a resistance dramatized by the use of stool-pigeons, agents provocateurs, blacklists, yellow-dog contracts, private police, strikebreakers fresh from prisons and gang killings, tear-gas and machine-gun arsenals, discharge of union sympathizers, promotion of tar-and-feather parties for union organizers, the corruption of judges and law-enforcement agencies, the formation of vigilante, good-citizen leagues and committees; in short, the lawless, irresponsible, antisocial, violent, un-American semi-feudal apparatus elaborately evolved by corporate enterprise for dealing with unionism.

But Green and his associates were soon disappointed. Employers on the whole—especially the bigger corporations in mass-production industry—remained as essentially anti-union as before. To evade the spirit, and conform to the letter of 7a they fashioned "company" unions, groups of workers bludgeoned or "advised" into belonging to an organization pledged, as a rule, in advance to dance with proper humility to all the tunes of management's piper.

At the same time employers refused to deal with the legitimate unions being formed either on an independent basis or as affiliates of the AFL. In midsummer 1933, workers in all parts of the country began to resent this cavalier treatment, especially after the newspapers had told them that the law was on their side. They started going out on strike: 139,000 of them in July, 211,000 in August, 298,000 in September—more than 700,000 during the last half of the year. And these strikes, the result of the social reform implicit in 7a, with its guarantee of labor's right to organize without interference from any source, collided with an equally important New Deal objective: business recovery. Hence President Roosevelt set up the National Labor

Board to mediate, arbitrate, conciliate, and otherwise resolve the differences arising between management and labor.

From the outset, however, the National Labor Board epitomized the New Deal's conflict between recovery and reform. The NRA administrators were anxious to secure co-operation from commerce and industry in formulating and operating the 585 different codes of fair competition. They were therefore inclined to soft-pedal any issue which might antagonize "business," especially such big business as motors and steel, the most virulently anti-union of all.

On the other hand, the National Labor Board, with its pro-union Senator Robert F. Wagner (D.,N.Y.) as chairman, interpreted 7a in accord with what it was meant to accomplish, and thus tended to aggravate some of the more autocratic tycoons into apoplexy, while some conservative papers began to predict barricades in the street.

Despite this nuisance value to labor, however, the Board was fundamentally weak. It was not equipped to enforce its own recommendations. It had to rely upon moral suasion and upon the weight of public opinion, scabbards without swords. Since its statutory status was in doubt, it had to become really a fact-finding commission which could inquire into alleged violations of 7a—chiefly employer attempts to thwart unionization, come hell or high water—and urge upon

27

management a greater indulgence in sweetness and light. But such concerns as Weirton Steel and Budd Manufacturing Company spurned Board decisions with impunity; and the Board was not staffed sufficiently to follow up the flouting of its orders or to handle the complaints that kept flooding its offices. Long, demoralizing delays ensued, while the bipartisan character of the Board, with its part employer, part labor personnel and its confusion of judicial and mediatory functions, merely combined maze with muddle.

Alarmed by this state of affairs, the AFL protested steadily until the National Labor Board was superseded in July 1934 by still another agency called the National Labor Relations Board (not to be confused with the present Board of the same title).

The new Board, created under Public Resolution 44, was made independent of the NRA set-up. It was given authority over all capital-labor controversy that might come up under 7a except steel, textiles, and the maritime industry, each of which had a special bureau all its own. At first it seemed as if this new Board would be able to go places and do things. It was composed of specialists in labor relations who cut red tape in all directions at once. Separated from the NRA, it was one step removed from the New Deal's liberal bloc, which favored unionism, and its conservative bloc, which believed in handing industry everything it asked for, and in double portions.

28

On the whole, however, this Board, too, failed to sur-
mount the difficulties which had plagued its predeces-
sor. For action against disobedient employers it had to
depend upon the Compliance Division of the NRA,
which would do everything for labor except give it a
break, and upon the Department of Justice, which
usually let labor complaint cases molder in a special
section of filing cabinets known, appropriately, as "the
morgue."

Yet the importance of this particular Board, as the
half-way house in the evolution of the New Deal's national labor policy, can hardly be overestimated. It carried forward the 7a mandate where its forerunner had
left off, and it also laid the groundwork for the present
National Labor Relations Board. It ruled, for example,
that the employer was not to demote or discharge workers in order to discourage their union affiliation. He
was further to reinstate employees fired for union activity, to refrain from financing company unions and
molesting outside unionists in their efforts to organize
his plant. In so far as the workers themselves were concerned, the Board held that whenever there was a question as to what union group—"company," or AFL, or
independent—should represent the employes of a given
mine, mill, or store, elections should be held and the
group obtaining the majority vote would then be certified as the appropriate collective-bargaining agency.
Finally, the Board insisted that once the spokesman for

29

the majority had been selected by this means, they should be "recognized" by the employer. It was not enough that he merely meet with them and discuss such non-essentials as paper towels in the locker-room; he must also bargain in good faith as to wages and hours and shop standards and exert every effort to reach an agreement in the form of a written contract, binding on both sides.

But in rendering such decisions and trying to give organized labor the "Clear track, go ahead" signal, the Board was constantly thwarted by that pernicious inertia which, for years, had been the occupational disease of most of AFL's officialdom.

II

THE passage of 7a and its aftermath, of course, evoked a widespread and spontaneous uprising of workers whose desire for unionism had been long repressed. But the Federation, with its ruling body, the Executive Council, dominated by the leaders of craft-type unions who clung fiercely to their narrow jurisdictional rights, failed to handle this vast new influx of the semi-skilled and unskilled labor with either vigor or vision. By the tens of thousands it placed eager new converts in federal labor unions, which are simply recruiting stations from which the various craft chieftains at their leisure siphon off anyone they can claim.

In Akron, for example, in the late summer of 1933, 4,500 rubber workers—inspired by two rank-and-file, home-grown leaders, Clark Culver and Fred Phillips— had organized themselves into an industrial union. They had adopted this style of organization, which is built around the product, as against the craft-type, which is built around skill, because it seemed the common-sense thing to do. They were all employed by the same firm; more than ninety-five per cent of them were unskilled and faced the same problems of highly mechanized mass-production industry. They applied to the AFL for a charter. Promptly from the Federation's headquarters in Washington, D. C., came Coleman Claherty, a veteran organizer of the old derby-wearing, "leave-it-to-me-boys" school. When he arrived in Akron, Claherty looked the situation over, nodded his head sadly, sagely. He had arrived, he said, in the nick of time. The big mistake, he pointed out to Messrs. Culver and Phillips, had been in setting up their new union on a plant-wide scale, instead of by the more sensible, longer-lasting craftwise method. Culver and Phillips admitted that they were novices, and asked for guidance. Claherty set to work. He talked to the men. He found out what their jobs entailed. Then, in accord with traditional AFL craft concepts, and despite the counter-evidence of conveyor-belts, he fashioned from this single all-embracing union, nineteen different and separate locals: viz.: Blacksmiths, Box Makers, Brick

Masons, Carpenters, Designers, Engineers, Electricians, Firemen, Machinists, Metal Workers, Mill Workers, Office Workers, Painters, Pipe Fitters, Plumbers, Printers, Sheet Metal Workers, Sign Painters, and Teamsters.

Under this new dispensation the members of each category were to wait and be assigned as ward to the AFL guardian to which they belonged by reason of "jurisdiction"; [1] in short, the Blacksmiths were turned over to the International Brotherhood of Blacksmiths, Drop Forgers and Helpers; and so on with all the rest up and down the line. Atrophy promptly set in, as in every similar case.

It was this partitioning process that accounted for the Federation's failure to capitalize fully on the union sentiment then sweeping the country. It explains also, in part, why the AFL's so-called craft unions in 1933–5 increased their enrollments only by 13 per cent while its four industrial unions gained 130 per cent, exactly ten times as much over the same period.

Yet the greater success of the industrial unions was due to more than their structural form. The once-in-a-lifetime opportunity offered to the AFL separated the quick from the dead among its chieftains, drawing a line between its labor leaders who were merely pro-

---

[1] In labor's language, jurisdiction is precisely what the dictionary says it is: "the lawful right to exercise official authority, whether executive, legislative or judicial."

32

fessional hacks and wheel-horses, and its leaders of labor who had spunk and energy and imagination. In the first category were the conservatives and in the second the liberals of the Federation; while a sprinkling of moderates, of men in between, composed perhaps another third of its officialdom.

Late in 1934, a restive insurgent group, representing about thirty-one per cent of the AFL membership, and led by John L. Lewis of the United Mine Workers, the AFL's biggest affiliate, began to insist that the industrial-union principle be applied to organizing mass-production workers. It contended that unless the Federation changed its tactics in this respect it would forfeit most, if not all, the advantages to be derived from the New Deal's assistance to unionism. It pointed out that mechanization, except in the building trades, printing, and a handful of others had reduced to uniform levels all but a few of the individual skills. It argued that in autos, radio, cement, glass, steel, and other mass-production spheres a worker often performed in the course of a day a half-dozen different tasks that would make him liable to jurisdictional claims of as many AFL unions. It claimed that in an era of the new technology, of the photo-electric eye, and the automatic cold strip rolling mill, and the like, it was simply stupid to adhere to the organizing techniques evolved for the semi-handicraft workshop of a bygone age.

33

The Lewis faction, which included both craft, industrial, and "mixed" unions, intended originally to convert a majority of the AFL members to this point of view and thus change Federation policy.

At the AFL 1934 convention in San Francisco, Lewis —aided particularly by the late Charles P. Howard, then president of the Typographers, one of the most successful craft-type unions in the Federation—centered discussion on the question of organizing policy. In the key resolutions committee he demanded that industrial-union charters be granted at once to aluminum, auto, cement, radio, and rubber workers. He maintained further that the task of unionizing of the steel industry should be removed from the inefficient, fumbling hands of Mike Tighe and his colleagues in the American Association of Iron, Steel and Tin Workers, which for years had stumbled along with a scant 7,700 members out of potentially more than 550,000. During five days of bitter intra-committee wrangling, John P. Frey, head of the AFL's Metal Trades Department, who for years had acted as the clark for the knights of craft unionism, argued for his proposal by which all organizers would be instructed that "under the laws and policies of the AFL wage-earners cannot be organized except into the respective national and international unions whose jurisdiction has been established." In other words, Frey said, even the federal union locals, which were directly affiliated with the national body of the AFL, should not be fashioned into industrial unions at any time, but rather their members should be surrendered to whatever craftsmen laid claim to them.

At this juncture Howard had to soothe Lewis down, while Matthew Woll, a moderate in the craft-industrial dispute, adroitly softened up Frey and his supporters until at long last a compromise was reached. It called for industrial charters in various mass-production and miscellaneous industries whenever the Executive Council might see fit. At the same time the council was entrusted with the job of defining the jurisdiction of all new unions, of appointing their officers and shaping their policies for a "provisional period," and of safeguarding the rights and priorities of the crafts. Moreover it was recommended that the council "shall at the earliest possible date inaugurate, manage, promote and conduct a campaign of organization in the steel industry." Finally, as a pledge of good faith, the council itself was to be enlarged and industrial-union leaders added to its predominantly craft membership.

Yet when this question reached the convention floor, craft stalwarts were suspicious of what any change in the status quo might do to them. Their apprehension was first expressed by William Hutcheson, hard-boiled, porcine, three-hundred-pound, bellowing czar of the Carpenters. For twenty years he had acted on the assumption that "God made the forests and then gave

35

them to Bill," a favorite joke among AFL initiates. He had taken the implications of this sentiment very seriously, however. He was, and to this day remains, convinced that he has a proprietary interest in all work done with wood in the United States, and that American institutions would be menaced if he shared this privilege with anyone else. His stand and all it implied was echoed by the lean, leathery, shrewd, part-Cherokee Arthur O. Wharton. His belief that "man is but a skill-hungry animal" was rooted in his fear that the 76,000 Machinists he commanded were so widely scattered among hundreds of different industries that they would be the first to be absorbed into industrial unions, destroying both his organization and his influence as its head.

Both Hutcheson and Wharton, and others like them, wanted to be assured, time after time, that no craft stronghold would be invaded, that no forays would be made among those whom they repeatedly described as "our men." And it was this possessive, paternalistic view—endemic among craft leaders especially—that inspired Andrew Furuseth, aging one-time president of the International Seamen's Union, to warn against the "new tyranny" that this narrow approach to unionism had often induced.

"I have heard many times in the labor movement," he declared, "the term 'these are my men.' A delegate or a labor council or someone who is sent out to organ-

ize says 'you are my men.' Who the devil is he? That
is the way the master talked for centuries of the slaves.
. . . And then along comes the employer and says, 'he
belongs to me; he is my employe. You mustn't interfere
with him, he is mine.' Is he? If he is, then our whole
civilization is a lie, our religion is a lie, our American
system of government is a lie. . . ."

He warned further against the tendency to make a
union into a tight little monopoly, with overtones of a
political machine, where the officers enjoyed a perpet-
uity of profits and prerogatives that set them adamantly
against new methods, new objectives in organization,
as potential threats to their own cushy positions.
The implications of his speech embarrassed altogether
too many of the delegates; and when he resumed his
seat, amid perfunctory applause, the convention moved
quickly to its close. The report of the resolutions committee was adopted by unanimous vote; and as a
further gesture of goodwill and honest intention the
importance of the industrial bloc was recognized by
electing to the Executive Council John L. Lewis of the
United Mine Workers, and David Dubinsky of the International Ladies' Garment Workers, heads of the two
largest industrial unions in the country.

The advocates of the "industrial idea," both within
and without the AFL, were jubilant over this apparent
victory for their cause. But their elation soon evapo-
rated. The presence of Lewis and Dubinsky in Execu-

tive Council deliberations after October 1934 was not enough to overcome its ingrained slothfulness. It was ten months before the council was prodded into giving the auto workers a limited industrial charter, and eleven before a similar privilege was conferred upon the rubber workers. Meanwhile valuable time was being lost. That first fine rapture in becoming a "union man," a desire which had swept spontaneously across the nation's industrial front, was turning into disillusionment and disgust. Workers who had joined the catch-all federal unions in the hope of getting action on their grievances were getting fed-up by the AFL's procrastination. They were eager and full of enthusiasm, but they were being compelled to wait in a state of animated suspense while, typically, in a Cincinnati radio factory five different crafts quarreled for three months over the allegiance of a single worker. Recent converts began tearing up or turning in their cards at an alarming rate.

From the standpoint of building a strong labor movement, of making hay under New Deal sunshine, the AFL simply wasn't functioning; at the very best it was traveling a mile when it could have gone ten. On the council Lewis and Dubinsky, as spokesmen for the industrial unionists, argued themselves hoarse in sessions marked by profanity, plain talk, and the seismic rumblings of future upheaval. They asserted that the do-nothing policy exemplified by the council was betraying the best interests of workers in general and the long-run welfare of the Federation in particular. They cited statistics on the ever increasing installation of labor-saving devices. They pled, Lewis thunderously, Dubinsky artfully. Both were unable to find a fulcrum with which to budge the opposition of craft die-hards, ever fearful that their job-control cartels might be menaced.

Yet this divergence in outlook, widening day by day, was rooted not only in personal stakes of various chieftains, but more fundamentally in the different economic conditioning of the contending factions.

The council was dominated by building-trades unions, which sell the bulk of their labor energy in a local market while the industrial unions sell their labor energy in a national market. A union bricklayer in Chicago who earns $1.50 an hour doesn't have his wage-scale directly menaced by the non-union bricklayer in Montgomery, Alabama, who is getting $.65 an hour. A building is not erected in Chicago for sale and shipment to somebody in Montgomery, or vice versa. The question of whether or not bricklaying labor is union or non-union is something that is settled locally with contractors who as a rule operate within the confines of a single city or county and even when they obtain out-of-town assignments do much, if not most, of their dealing with local labor.

On the other hand, the soft-coal miner in Virden,

Illinois, who earns 90 cents an hour has reason to be worried by his equivalent, in Birmingham, Alabama, who is receiving half that amount. Their commodity is sold in a national market. From 5,200 tipples in twenty-six states, from Kentucky to Utah, from Colorado to Virginia, bituminous coal is transported to New York, New Orleans, San Francisco. Often enough coal mined within a stone's throw of Chicago is delivered to customers in Montgomery, and the other way round.

Under these circumstances, as the United Mine Workers learned from years of disheartening experience, if you expect to maintain union rates of pay you have to organize a substantial majority of mines on a uniform basis, to stabilize the industry before you can keep a stable union within it. Otherwise the chiseler is going to undersell the operator who is maintaining union wages and hours. The United Mine Workers long ago discovered that it could not expect the cooperative employer to be constantly undercut in his prices and placed at a competitive disadvantage and still meet its demands. There comes a day when he refuses to sign any contract with the union unless his rivals are bound by virtually the same terms. The essentials of this policy of course had proved to be as crucially necessary for stable effective unionism in women's wear and men's clothing as in coal-mining.

By much the same token the primary political emphasis of the building trades has been municipal.

The Carpenters, Plumbers, Hod-Carriers were interested in city administrations which could be influenced to issue permits to contractors who employed union labor. The Miners and Garment Workers were primarily interested in state and national legislation that would help to eliminate health hazards on the job, and cut-throat competition within, the industries where they moved and had their being. And because the nature of mining and manufacturing compelled them to think and act on a nation-wide, as against a local, basis, the latter perceived more acutely than their opponents that the open shop anywhere was a constant threat to union standards everywhere.

The industrial group also had accepted, tentatively at least, the thesis that to flourish, even to exist, under present-day conditions, unions needed not only economic organization but also the ability to direct votes for governors and congressmen and presidents who would continue to look upon labor as a sentient integer in the American equation, rather than as an inanimate commodity. And the best way to achieve this objective, Lewis and his colleagues believed, was to organize the unorganized, especially in mass-production areas, and to educate them into political consciousness so that at the polls labor would be a force with which both politicians and statesmen would have to reckon.

The clash between the immovable object of labor's older localism and the irresistible force of its newer na-

41

tionalism (along with other elements to be considered later) resulted in the great and tragic division in the American labor movement which occurred at the AFL's Atlantic City convention in October 1935.

The Lewis alignment entered the convention auditorium in a grim and bellicose mood. They had been sold out, they believed. The promises exacted at San Francisco a year before had remained only a paper triumph. They were ready to risk a show-down fight, even prematurely, with the odds against them.

Once more the vital resolutions committee was racked by disagreement as the craft-versus-industrial argument sharpened into bitter stubborn conflict. What was vague a year before was now etched in acid, what had been polite was now without gloves. Among the twenty-one resolutions examined by the committee, nine called for the immediate issuance of industrial charters in specific industries and twelve asked that various craft unions be promptly supplanted by the industrial form of organization.

In the majority report, eight members of the committee, led by John P. Frey, opposed industrial unionism as embodied in these proposals, seeking to curtail any broad application of the San Francisco program. He affirmed that the 1934 statement had been "misunderstood." In the automotive industry, for example, he drew a strict distinction between "mass-production" workers along a conveyor belt and those in accessory and parts factories, although the mechanization in the latter is quite as intense as in assembly plants.

Whereas this separation of sheep from goats didn't make much sense in the abstract, it would serve to protect the claims of the Machinists, which had enlisted quite a few members in accessory and parts establishments. And to substantiate his interpretation Frey quoted at length from the 1934 declaration: "We consider it our duty . . . to protect the jurisdictional rights of all trade unions organized upon craft lines and afford them every opportunity for development of accession of those workers engaged upon work over which these organizations have jurisdiction." And to clinch this point he further said that the AFL in its San Francisco statement had merely revalidated the "contracts" mutually assumed between the Federation and its craft affiliates during the last two decades of the nineteenth century. He concluded therefore that to grant to the industrial union the latitude desired by its sponsors would be simply to violate these agreements. "The American Federation of Labor," he proclaimed, "could not have been organized upon any other basis of relationship. It is recognized that where a contract is entered into between parties, it cannot be set aside or altered by one party without the consent and approval of the other. . . ."

The minority report, presented by Charles P. Howard, was the complete converse of the Frey findings. It urged the AFL to encourage mass-production workers to build industrial unions and to receive "unrestricted charters" which would "guarantee the right to accept into membership all workers employed in the industry." At the same time Howard asserted: "It is not the intention of this declaration of policy to permit the taking away from . . . craft unions any part of their present membership, or potential membership, in establishments where the dominant factor is skilled craftsmen. . . ." And as a corollary Howard suggested that the Executive Council should embark upon a campaign of winning over "company-dominated unions" by giving them also unrestricted charters, which, of course, would exclude craft unions from such predominantly mass-production spheres as autos, electrical appliances, cement, glass, steel and radio.

In the days of debate that followed the submission of these two at loggerheads reports, Philip Murray, vicepresident of the United Mine Workers, and Marshal Ney to Lewis's Napoleon, assailed the Executive Council for its failure to do anything intelligent or effective about organizing steel. He reminded the convention that steel workers in the Aliquippa and Ambridge regions of Pennsylvania had fashioned an up-and-coming industrial union, on their own, against all the handicaps in the book. They had enrolled 6,500 out of a potential 8,000, although the moving spirits of this enterprise were never quite sure that they would get home alive when they set forth for a secret meeting, what with the marksmanship of company police and the presence of many stool-pigeons. And these new unionists, Murray said, proud of their achievement, asked the AFL for a charter. The crafts—aided by the Executive Council—responded with "business as usual." They dispatched their own organizers, who with great diligence broke up this nascent steel union into nine different parts, destroying the sense of solidarity so patiently nursed, while the usual atrophy began setting in. "And now," declared Murray, accusingly, "they have no organization, they have no charter, they have no independent union, they have no craft union. They are today where they were before they started their campaign eighteen months ago. . . ."

Despite such evidence, the veracity of which nobody challenged, Daniel Tobin of the Teamsters defied the "very gates of hell" to prevail against labor's rock of ages, the "rock of crafts' autonomy, craft trades." He envisioned the AFL's Founding Fathers, P. J. McGuire and Samuel Gompers, as "spirits" which "must writhe in persecution and misery listening to the charges and counter-charges (on the part of John L. Lewis) that this Federation of Labor has been twenty-five years of continuous failure." The entire industrial-union movement, Tobin declaimed, was really "an attempt to de-

45

stroy the very foundations upon which this Federation has been builded and upon which it has succeeded for years."

Nor did Lewis's baroque but brilliant rhetoric dissuade the majority of his audience from the Tobin point of view, although many of the five hundred delegates afterwards declared that the address of the Miners' chieftain was the best they had ever heard.

The new unions, said Lewis, were "dying like the grass before the autumn sun." "Why not," he asked, "make a contribution to the well-being of those who are not fortunate enough to be members of your organizations? The labor movement is organized upon the principle that the strong shall help the weak. Is it right, after all, that because some of us are capable of forging great and powerful unions of skilled craftsmen . . . we should lock ourselves up in our domain and say, 'I am merely working for those who pay me'? Isn't it right that we should contribute something of our own strength, our own knowledge, our own influence toward those less fortunately situated" if only because "if we help them and they grow strong, in turn we will be the beneficiaries of their changed status and their strength.

"The strength of a strong man," he continued, "is a prideful thing, but the unfortunate thing in life is that strong men do not remain strong. And that is just as true of unions and labor organizations. And whereas today the craft unions may be able to stand upon their own feet, and like mighty oaks before the gale, defy the lightning, the day may come when this changed scheme of things—and things are rapidly changing now —when these organizations will not be able to withstand the lightning and the gale. . . . Prepare yourselves by making a contribution now to your less fortunate brethren. . . . Organize the unorganized and in doing this make the American Federation of Labor the greatest instrument . . . to befriend the cause of humanity and champion human rights. . . ."

Yet despite Lewis's eloquence the test vote on the motion to accept the minority report of the industrial unionists was lost by a tally of 18,024 to 10,933.

And the day after the convention had been formally adjourned, nine labor chieftains—John L. Lewis, Philip Murray, John Brophy, Thomas Kennedy of the United Mine Workers; Sidney Hillman of the Amalgamated Clothing Workers, Thomas McMahon of the United Textile Workers, Max Zaritsky of the Hat, Cap and Millinery Workers, Charles P. Howard of the Typographers, and David Dubinsky of the International Ladies' Garment Workers held a seven-hour session at the Hotel President in Atlantic City and verbally gave birth to the Committee for Industrial Organization.

On November 9, 1935 in Washington, D. C., this group, already enlarged by the addition of Thomas Brown of the Mine, Mill and Smelter Workers and Harvey Fremming of the Oil Field, Gas, Well and

Refinery Workers, officially launched the first CIO It intended to function strictly as a special committee within the AFL. Its purpose, said its sponsors, was "to encourage and promote organization of the workers in the mass production and unorganized industries" and to affiliate them with the AFL. It was going to be "educational and advisory," and its chairman was Lewis, its secretary Howard, its executive director Brophy.

Some two weeks after the formation of the CIO, William Green expressed to its components his "apprehension and deep concern" lest the CIO become a "dual" movement, a rival of the AFL. He insisted that the genuine issue was not craft-versus-industrial unionism, but that of majority rule; that the question of organizational form should continue to be threshed out before the AFL's legislative body, its annual convention, since the democratic process made it mandatory for a minority to abide by majority decision.

But the CIO leaders were dubious about the AFL's devotion to the democratic process. "It is not unethical or improper," Howard replied to Green, "for a minority to have its proposals adopted by the majority by proper discussion . . . and by an effort to convert those whose interests are most affected—the rank and file of workers. To confine the effort to conventions . . . would be to presume that only officers and delegates are to be considered. . . . My experience does not justify acceptance of such a restriction. . . . During

48

the years I have been a delegate to AFL conventions, I have observed the strongest cohesion in a controlling group for the purpose of determining every question. . . . Some of us have had the conclusion forced upon us that the merits of proposals are not the determining factor in rendering decisions. . . ."

He later reiterated that the CIO would not depart from the resolution at San Francisco in 1934, the intent of which had been negated by "unsympathetic interpretation and administration" by the Executive Council. Since he had prepared that particular report, he added, he knew what it had aimed to accomplish, and that, and that alone, was what the CIO was going to do. It was not going to create a new federation of labor. It was not going to "raid" the membership of already existing unions. Its entire *raison d'être* was to "organize the un-organized."

"Dear Sir and Brother," said Lewis in a letter to Green on November 23, 1935, "Effective this date I resign as vice-president of the American Federation of Labor." And when the Executive Council gathered in special session in Miami early in January 1936, it was further shocked to receive from the CIO a request that industrial-union charters be granted at once to auto and rubber workers and to the independent National Radio union, and that a campaign be immediately undertaken in steel.

In reply the council demanded that the CIO "be

immediately dissolved" since its very existence was a "challenge to the supremacy of the Federation." It refused to give an industrial charter to radio workers, offering them instead a class-b (non-voting) status within the Electricians' union. It assigned to Wharton's Machinists the right to absorb all workers in automotive parts and accessory plants and decided to unionize the rest of the motor industry along lines partly craft and partly industrial.

From that point forward, events rushed toward a cacophonous climax. In Washington late in January the United Mine Workers in convention voted to withhold $48,000 in per capita dues to the AFL treasury, while Philip Murray received an ovation when he remarked: "I say to you as an officer of the United Mine Workers of America, the sooner we get to hell away from there [the AFL] the better off we will be." Simultaneously in Toledo the Federation of Flat Glass Workers approved the CIO plan to guide expansion in their field on an industrial basis. In Philadelphia the radio workers rejected the AFL demand that they be merged into the Brotherhood of Electrical Workers. On the 20th of February Green ordered 1,354 local and federal unions, 49 state federations (the extra one was for the District of Columbia), and 730 city centrals to regard the CIO as "verboten."

In April the CIO had already begun to ingest the decadent Amalgamated Association of Steel, Iron and

Tin Workers, for whose allegiance it outmaneuvered the AFL. Shunting the Amalgamated's doddering officers like freight-cars to the sidings, the CIO collected $500,000 for an energetic drive in the steel industry under the direction of the immensely able Philip Murray, chairman of the CIO's Steel Workers' Organizing Committee.

More than anything else yet attempted by the CIO, this campaign alarmed the Executive Council. It foresaw that if the CIO attained any genuine measure of success in this undertaking, it would be so much strengthened in prestige and numbers that at the next AFL convention in November it would be able to defy with impunity any efforts to discipline its unorthodox behavior. On June 30, therefore, the council ordered the ten CIO unions to appear before it on July 7 and refute, if they could, the charge that they were fostering a movement of insurrection and rebellion. Otherwise, said the council, it would suspend all the CIO affiliates.

The CIO ignored the summons; the deadline date passed and none of the accused showed up. The AFL tried again. It asked the CIO, which, with the accession of the Auto and Rubber Workers early in July, now had twelve affiliates, to be present for trial on August 3. The CIO refused to appear. Instead it pointed out to the council that its suspension, in whole or in part, would be utterly illegal since to suspend was tantamount to expulsion, and that under Article IX, Section 12, of the AFL Constitution the ability to expel any affiliate was expressly reserved to a two-thirds vote of the Federation's annual convention.

What the CIO didn't know, however, was that in May the Executive Council, by means of a legalistic procedure still surrounded by darkness, had invested itself with a new "implied power" by which it could sit as a court to hear charges of "breach of contract" between the AFL and its unions, to hold "trials" on such charges, and to suspend the defendants if found guilty. Hence on August 4, 1936 the CIO unions were ejected by a vote of 13 to 1 on the double count of creating a "dual" or competing movement and of refusing to comply with the "cease and desist" fiat of the Executive Council and were given a month, until September 5, to change their minds. But this ouster served only to stiffen the morale of the CIO, and no signs of repentance were visible as the day marking labor's new separatism came and went.

Then in November, in Tampa, the fifty-sixth annual convention of the AFL ratified the Executive Council's action by a 21,679 to 2,043 vote; but the impressive effect of this total was marred by the absence of the CIO and was merely a case of a craft-controlled convention vindicating a craft-controlled Executive Council. For it should be remembered that in Tampa the CIO was not officially represented. Whatever spokes-

men it had were old-time friends like the Brewery
Workers and the Bakers, and some "observers," who
were at best ambassadors with neither country nor
portfolio. It should also be recalled that the AFL had
its die-hards and moderates in key positions even as
the absentee CIO. The array of opposing forces, as
exemplified by their central figures, resulted in a rare
amount of fanfare and fulmination, for the implications of the impending split were beginning to concern
leaders on both sides.

Participating in this melee even by remote control
and through the agency of intermediaries were the
CIO die-hards Lewis and Howard and Hillman. And,
contrary to the widespread impression that the needle-
trades chieftains like Hillman, Dubinsky, and Zaritsky
always see eye to eye, the fracas divided this trinity
with Hillman (who has been in and out of the AFL)
as adamant as Lewis, while Dubinsky and Zaritsky
joined with McMahon of the Textile Workers to carry
the standard for the CIO moderates. In the AFL camp
Wharton of the Machinists, Coefield of the Plumbers,
Tobin of the Teamsters were the dominant die-hards,
with William Hutcheson lending aid and counsel.
William Green and Matthew Woll, the latter less
firmly, took their stand with the AFL moderates, seeking to help George M. Harrison of the Railway Clerks
and Felix Knight of the Railway Carmen to achieve
Armistice instead of Armageddon.

First off, to justify its totally illegal act of suspension, the Executive Council called upon Matthew Woll, who is an attorney. It was an assignment that even the fanciest corporation lawyer would have shunned; for the plain meaning of the English language has rarely had to be so tortured and twisted to serve a partisan cause.

"It is true," Woll admitted, "that nowhere specifically is the Executive Council authorized to suspend. . . . But necessarily, in the absence of any specific provision we must fall back to the doctrines adopted in all organizations, in all voluntary movements, accepted by courts, and universally as the practice; and that is the doctrine of assumed and implied considerations. And what is meant by that?"

He didn't know, actually, but he kept pitching until the players, the umpire, and the fans couldn't follow the ball. He said that there was a difference between suspending a union and expelling it. In the first instance you debarred it from privileges, and in the second you drove it out. He neglected to mention, however, that practically in labor affairs to suspend and to expel are one and the same thing; for a union once cut off from the support of the national body and its constituent unions exists on another plane altogether.

He next considered Section 8 of Article 12 in the AFL Constitution, which states that the Executive

Council "shall only have power to revoke the charter" when this "has been ordered by a two-thirds majority of the convention." And presumably invoking the spirit of John Marshall, Woll declared: "All this does not say the convention shall have the power to revoke, either by majority or by two-thirds vote, and still the question is open whether the convention may not, of its own accord, revoke a charter by majority vote."

And while newsmen, covering the convention, went goggle-eyed over this gibberish, Woll continued: "Section 8 is but a limitation, a restriction, not a grant, upon its [the council's] powers, and it can only exercise the power of revocation [expulsion] when the convention authorizes it to do so by a two-thirds vote. Now, the Executive Council, having been vested with this greater power of revocation, specifically limited by the convention . . . *it follows that it had the power to suspend without further recommendation or limitation, because the Constitution is completely silent on that point*" (italics mine).

When he had finished with this constitutional *coup d'état,* Woll suffered a nervous collapse and was confined to a hospital bed for several days. And this was understandable enough. Woll fundamentally is honest, and his performance on this occasion must have provoked all the agonizing inner conflict of a man who, to carry out an assignment, forces himself to rationalize rather than to think straight. After all, Woll is ex-

55

tremely intelligent, he is the chief logician of the Gompers gospel. He has modified, even modernized, the precepts of "voluntarism," but its core remains for him labor's only true and proper credo. In this respect he belongs to the old guard, which dies on its conclusions rather than surrender on its premises. Even the outmoded style of his attire, his wing-collar, his bowtie, his contrivings to resemble a daguerreotype of a turn-of-the-century beau, with the latter's over-formalized speech, are but the corporeal features of his loyalty to a viewpoint archaic, yet alluring. Formerly head of the Photo-Engravers Union, currently president of the Union Life Insurance Company, specializing in a labor clientele, Woll is by training a lawyer, by avocation a businessman, and by preference and occupation an elder of the AFL tribe, who walks backward into the future. His word-jugglings at Tampa were only in part the doing of a distasteful chore at the Executive Council's behest; they were in large measure inspired by his desire to shut out reality, to replace it by the sentimental cravings of a labor Conrad in Quest of his Youth.

And though nobody quite understood what Woll had been talking about, the intention was taken for performance, and the delegates with audible relief felt that the question had been somehow disposed of and turned to the real business at hand: a complete break or complete conciliation with the CIO. In this regard the AFL die-hards wanted a total victory, a victor's victory with all the trophies of conquest hanging from their shields. They demanded the technical expulsion of the CIO unions, a final closing of the door. They spurned attempts at rapprochement as signs of cowardice. They were still rankling under the CIO bloc's none too subtle inferences that they were at once shortsighted, selfish, and outmoded. And similarly among the CIO warriors the die-hards maintained that any compromise was impossible unless three basic conditions were met: (1) that the suspensions be immediately lifted; (2) that provisions be made for an intensive and genuine nation-wide drive for industrial unionism; and (3) that the AFL Constitution be amended to deprive the Executive Council from usurping authority to suspend any affiliate for any reason.

On the other hand, both AFL and CIO moderates sought peace at almost any price. They were ready to make concessions. They were willing to put forth mutually face-saving stratagems as fast as they could be invented. But, like most moderates in any crisis, they were hoisted by the petard of their own reasonableness.

For ten days that shook America's labor world, the debates and jockeyings for position between the AFL and the CIO continued by telephone and telegraph, by lobbyings and whisperings, by coded memoranda and confidential messengers, by trial-balloon discussions in

57

secret hotel-room meetings, and in the press. While on the floor of the convention no fireworks were exploded, the behind-the-scenes activity resembled, in scope and intensity, the cabals and plottings of the 1920 Republican National Convention which conjured up Harding and back-to-normalcy out of a smoked-filled room.

In Washington John L. Lewis, who wanted a quick clean break, kept sending provocative telegrams to William Green to prod him into the retaliatory action instead of his fluttering verbal responses. In Miami, like Sheridan twenty miles away, David Dubinsky, who was to assume the role of perennial peacemaker, champed on his stubby cigars, his ear glued to a phone, ready to rush upon the scene of action should a propitious occasion arise. And in Tampa itself the ailing Charles P. Howard, CIO secretary, in a state of indecision, sulked like Achilles in his tent, not once setting foot in the convention hall though he remained in town for many days, and his hotel was but a few blocks distant from the battle-front.

Despite all these advances and withdrawals, the whole contest became a game nobody won. There was only inning after inning of no hits, no runs, no errors. The AFL die-hards didn't expel the CIO, and the moderates on both sides were given nothing tangible with which they might bargain to keep the CIO within the Federation, but obtained only the cheer residing in such phrases as "There is room enough for all, honor enough for all," and "United we stand, divided we fall." But even these platitudes brought little comfort when placed alongside the decision to keep the suspensions in force until the "breach be healed and adjusted under such terms and conditions as the Executive Council may deem best."

In March 1937, as the CIO was moving like a Roman legion battering down citadel after citadel of the open shop in steel, autos, glass, rubber, and other mass-production spheres, bringing unionism to a thousand places where it was merely a pious hope before, the AFL instructed all its city centrals and state federations to expel anyone who belonged to a CIO union. And over the protests of more than half a million AFL rank-and-file members this order was executed with an alertness that showed that at long last the AFL's officials, major and minor, were astir, and moving about with the instinctive celerity of organisms whose food supply is threatened by a more energetic member of the same species.

In altogether too many cases the heads of locals and secondary and tertiary business agents left their swivel chairs long enough to carry out the ejection of CIO adherents by the steam-roller methods of the ward boss. And once on their feet, all the AFL leaders had to get on their toes, and stay there, to offset the hard-hitting rivalry of the CIO, its daring, its gumption, its magnificent accomplishments. Within the AFL hundreds of leaders who for years had done nothing more arduous than collect their pay-checks now had to get out and hustle, to "keep the boys in line"; for the CIO example of doing something for its members was too public not to be contagious.

Meanwhile the CIO, hitting back at the Federation's purge of members from the city and state alignments, began to form similar bodies of its own, calling them industrial councils. At the same time, at a special conference in Cincinnati on May 24, the AFL decided to increase the per capita tax of its loyal unions from one cent to two cents a month. The extra penny per member was to be used to forestall the CIO, wherever possible, and to enlarge the AFL by more intense organizing activity, the second more as a function of the first. That this double purpose was celestial the AFL did not doubt, nor did its president.

"The first dual movement," William Green intoned on this occasion, "occurred in heaven itself, a place where harmony and peace prevailed. Yet a dual movement began," he went on, "when as a committee of one, Michael the Archangel rebelled against God and His authority. The executive council in heaven did not hesitate to act. After examining the facts, it expelled his Satanic Majesty and his dual movement from heaven."

And in June, in retaliation for the AFL's intensifying of hostilities, the devil's disciples, until then financed by voluntary contributions, mainly from the miners and the clothing and women's-wear workers, inaugurated their own system of per capita payments.

The division in the American labor movement was now complete.

When in October 1938, at its first constitutional convention in Pittsburgh, the first CIO transformed itself from a temporary committee into a permanent Congress of Industrial Organizations, it but formally recognized what for two years had been a *fait accompli*.

CHAPTER III

CRAFT VERSUS INDUSTRIAL ORGANIZATION: FACT INTO MYTH

DURING THE four and a half years that the increasingly bitter competition between the AFL and the CIO has widened the gap in labor's ranks, it has made meaningless the original cause of the cleavage: the contest between craft and industrial forms of organization.

In the maritime industry alone, the CIO has chartered four important craft unions,[1] while the AFL, not to be outdone, has chartered new industrial unions in coal- and metal-mining[2] and in various other spheres.

In order to make sense out of this seeming paradox,

[1] They are: International Union of Fishermen's and Allied Workers; the National Association of Marine Cooks and Stewards; the National Marine Engineers Beneficial Association; and the Inland Boatmen's Union of the Pacific.

[2] The Progressive Mine Workers of America and the Tri-State Metal, Mine and Smelter Workers.

examine for a moment the few simple and basic tenets of American union structure, which provide a key to a perplexing problem.

While as a short cut the use of the term "craft" (or "crafts") union is often necessary, and even unavoidable, it describes only the general and generic rather than the specific and current attributes of a whole category of different union forms. It is pertinent therefore to define what a craft union actually is and what it means both in labor's lexicon and in American industry today.

You can search the constitutions and charters of the 102 unions affiliated with the AFL, and put your magnifying glass over the small print of clause 44-b of subsection 21-k of the by-laws, and find absolutely nothing to help you in this quest. Nor has the Federation's G.H.Q. any standard official definition.

Indeed, late in 1939, in testifying before a Senate committee on proposed changes in the National Labor Relations Act, the able and astute Joseph Padway, general counsel for the AFL, declined to specify what a craft union consists of—chiefly on the ground of "technological improvements." He seemed to regard it as an act of faith.

It is more than that, however. It exists. In its purest pristine form it exists as the *single craft union* which comprises workers who have the same kind of training and the same kind of skill, each one of whom can carry through—from start to finish—a particular whole process of production.

In this respect consider the work done by the AFL Wood Carvers, practitioners of an ancient and honorable craft, with antecedents going back to the medieval guilds and beyond.

Suppose that in downtown Manhattan a restaurant-owner who has many Anglophile patrons desires to remodel his grill-room into a replica of the interior of an old English tavern. He decides that over the fireplace he particularly wants a wooden plaque of Britannia's national seal, with the lion and unicorn rampant and all the rest of it.

He consults with his decorator, who in turn draws a sketch of the idea and brings it to a wood-carving establishment, where the manager assigns the execution of this design to one of five or six wood-carvers, whose skills, be it observed, are identical and interchangeable. Perhaps he selects Henry Briggs. Now, Briggs must have served four solid years of apprenticeship before he has been allowed to do anything on his own. He must be able to handle with delicate precision such tools as the straight and bent gouges, chisels, the spade, the wooden mallet, and many more. The palm of his hand is his "hammer." His thumb and index finger require the digital dexterity of a pianist playing a Chopin étude. He must know thoroughly such tricks of the trade as that pine, being a soft wood, needs a sharper edge on cutting instruments than the harder oak. He studies the pattern for the plaque, he confers with both the decorator and the manager, and translates it carefully from paper into wood. He does it himself. He is on his own. He is a skilled craftsman in the sense of the term that had special meaning and significance when the AFL was founded, fifty-nine years ago, when its coopers, its molders, its top-hatted, frock-coated rollers and melters of steeldom's labor aristocracy also belonged to the single craft category now occupied by a Henry Briggs and a handful of his prototypes.

For in the 1940's the wood-carver, the wire-weaver, the sheep-shearer, the horseshoer, and a few others alone constitute this single craft grouping, and they make up at most 27,000 out of the more than 4,000,000 total membership of the Federation, or slightly more than one quarter of one per cent. And it is solely in this classification that the CIO has no affiliates.

The year 1881 not only marked the birth of the AFL but also witnessed the beginnings of the "new great period of growth" in American business. By the score new industries arose, flourished, expanded. During the next three decades the workshop and small factory gave way, at a rapid rate, before the big corporation that fused many separate enterprises into trusts, which, as in the case of United States Steel, were again merged into something bigger still. The forward sweep of science and invention introduced more and more mechanization, especially into manufacturing, erasing many old skills, creating a new division and subdivision of labor, and bringing a new complexity and a new diversity to the American scene.

Under the impact of these trends three different things happened to the single craft union. A very few, like the wood-carvers, operating always in a limited field, remained relatively undisturbed by the epoch's innovations. Others, like the carriage-makers, who formed the first labor force in the automobile factories of such pioneers as Ford and Haynes and Duryea, had dwindled into virtual extinction during the first World War.

Yet more often the single craft union was combined with others in the same occupational sector to become the *compound* or *amalgamated* or *multi-crafts* union of the present day.

At the turn of the century, for example, the use of new methods like the cement gun, and of new materials like concrete flooring, caused the work of the bricklayer, the stone-mason, and the plasterer to overlap as never before. In many cases it was impossible to tell where the function of the first began, where the second ended, where the third fitted in, if at all. Yet all three crafts were needed in building a cafeteria, a Colonial mansion, a cathedral. All three maintained separate unions of their own, and difficulties ensued over the question of what job belonged to whom. In 1910, however, to avoid the troubles arising from such dilemmas as who deserved to apply that newfangled substance, stucco, which was neither brick nor stone nor plaster, these three single crafts merged themselves into today's International Union of Bricklayers, Masons and Plasterers. And six years later, when this organization was affiliated with the AFL, the latter—to sidestep jurisdictional rows—made it a present of authority over the marble-setters, whose jobs were encroaching upon the domain of bricklayer, mason, and plasterer alike.

As early as 1901, in fact, the AFL in its famous Scranton Declaration affirmed that in view of the "recent great changes in production and employment" the welfare of the labor movement "will be promoted by closely allying the subdivided crafts," without, however, making "any radical departure from" the "fundamental principle" of "organization on trade lines."

And by 1912 the Executive Council proudly reported that it had reduced a great deal of friction among various unions by linking the metal mechanics with the machinists, blending the woodworkers with the carpenters, the lasters with the boot and shoe workers, the granite-rubbers and sawyers with the cutters, and by otherwise nurturing the development of the compound or multi-crafts union.

The quite recent evolution of "barbering" is still another illustration of this same practice. Formerly all a barber shop needed was a barber, or two or three or more, along with a candy-stick pole, initialed mugs, chairs, razors, cuspidors, and a calendar depicting some voluptuously convex wench in the nude. But with the modern tendency toward the tonsorial Taj Mahal and beauty salon, more and more under the same roof, there has come a vast array of new gadgets and appliances and customs. In any such establishment personnel is composed not only of barbers but also of marcellers, wavers, cosmeticians, hairdressers, manicurists, and others. The Journeymen Barbers Union [1] includes them all. Unlike the wood-carver's, their skills are neither identical nor interchangeable. Yet all are required to conduct this kind of business with profit and efficiency. In this compound or multi-craft division the AFL has thirty-three and the CIO nine unions in good standing.

Nor is this somewhat surprising situation any different when the two great intermediary types of American unionism, the *semi-industrial* and the *trade*, are examined in the light both of their structure and of their allegiance.

On the whole, both semi-industrial and trade unions are outgrowths of the compound or multi-crafts in much the same manner that these have ramified from the single-craft nucleus.

[1] The CIO has recently started a Barbers Organizing Committee to rival this fifty-year-old affiliate of the AFL.

The *semi-industrial* union, however, has control over the basic occupations of a *whole* industry, skilled, semi-skilled, and unskilled, excluding only the auxiliary tasks. The United Hat, Cap and Millinery Workers (AFL) is an excellent illustration of this point. It is almost all-embracing except for workers engaged in maintenance—that is, the mechanics, electricians, painters, who are responsible for the repair of machinery and the general physical upkeep of the plant.

The *trade* union, on the other hand, covers skilled, semi-skilled, and unskilled, true enough, but only for a particular *part* of an industry. Thus the Printing Pressmen admits roller-makers, carriers, newsboys, and paper-handlers in addition to its primary printing and offset artisans. But it does not include all the workers within the confines of printing as a vocation, such as the typographers, the photo-engravers, the stereotypers, and the like.

The AFL has twenty-nine semi-industrial unions and nineteen trade unions. The CIO has six semi-industrial and four trade unions.

And at the center of the whole *Sturm und Drang* over labor's organizing modes and manners is the industrial union, object of lavish acclaim and even more lavish acrimony, the polemicist's paradise over the past four years.

The *industrial* union includes literally "everybody," in the pit, at the loom, along the conveyor belt, or whatever. The classic example, of course, is the United Mine Workers, backbone of the CIO for more than four years and the chief vertebra of the AFL for forty-two years. The United Mine Workers, in its statement of jurisdiction, simply claims "all workers in and around the mines," including engineers and firemen and pump-runners as well as coal miners of varying degrees. The Progressive Miners of the AFL is set up along exactly the same lines.[1]

Although the Federation has only ten industrial unions, they are numerically the biggest group within the AFL, totaling about 855,000 persons, or almost 25 per cent of its entire enrollment—as compared with the CIO's industrial affiliates, whose claimed 3,000,000 or over adherents comprise nearly 75 per cent of its whole membership.

Necessarily, union structure is constantly in flux, changing from day to day to correspond to new tools, new machines, new processes in industry; for fundamentally union forms follow the trends of technology —sometimes slowly, sometimes rapidly, but always and inevitably over any given period. All distinctions are

[1] The main reason why coal-mining unions are wholly industrial is that collieries as a rule are the single industry in an isolated community. From the beginnings of the AFL, the craft unions didn't think it worth while, in time or money, to try to enlist a mere handful of potential recruits among the coal mine's carpenters, machinists, and the like. Hence the Scranton Declaration permitted craftsmen in such areas to join the "paramount" organization.

therefore somewhat arbitrary, and boundary lines often blur.

The difficulty of formulating any strictly rigid rule is exemplified by the versatile United Brotherhood of Carpenters and Joiners (AFL). In building construction it acts sometimes as a compound crafts and sometimes as a trade union. In a furniture factory it is semi-industrial. In a logging camp it is one-hundred-per-cent industrial. And ironically enough the Brotherhood, which has gone on record as being vigorously opposed to any embodiment of the "industrial idea," is, in its own far-reaching and varied activity, that kind of supra-special industrial union technically known as "*vertical.*"

The Brotherhood is built around a commodity—wood. It reserves to itself the right to work with wood (and even wood substitutes) in almost all of its manifestations, from tree to log, from lumber to parquetry. And in its tremendous scope—from raw material to finished product—it cuts across many different kinds of industry, making modest by comparison the claims of the ordinary, more readily recognized type of industrial union like those in rubber, glass, or cement.

Certainly today two basic and inescapable conclusions would seem to emerge from any impartial survey of union contours and coloration. The first is that there is nothing inherently superior in the abstract in

71

either the craft or the industrial mode of organization. Both are needed in all their gradations. Both reflect the character and customs of the industrial countries they inhabit. Both are shaped by external influences such as (among many others) the extent to which labor-saving devices are installed and used, and the period of training required for a particular occupation.

In the province of large-scale mass production it would by now seem axiomatic that the industrial union is organically best adapted to the worker's need. In motors, where the assembly-line technique has reached its American apogee, both R. J. Thomas's CIO United Automobile Workers Union and the Federation's Automobile Workers Union are compelled perforce to act upon this assumption, despite some minor craft "raids" upon the latter attempted by the Machinists.

With the perhaps 1.5-per-cent exception of the extremely expert tool- and die-makers and a few others (who often protect their higher wage-scales by means of a separate local within the industrial union) the average wage-earner learns his job in three or four weeks. He sets a fender perhaps, and does it steadily, for eight hours, and nothing else; or he performs similar repetitive tasks fitting no craft category. Often he tends a machine that intricately integrates many different operations formerly done by hand—thus inviting the jurisdictional claims of seven or eight different crafts, but rendering ridiculous any effort to enforce the claim of one against any other.

Under such circumstances his collective-bargaining strength depends not upon his ownership of a specific and relatively scarce skill, but upon his close collaboration with his fellows, with all of them, to maintain or improve his wages and to humanize his job. As an individual owning only his own willingness to work he hasn't a prayer should he, even in conjunction with a small group of others, try to buck the impersonal might —social, political, legal, economic—of a multi-million- or billion-dollar corporation. But as one of thousands of individuals, acting in concert on the basis of common interests and a common cause, and able to withdraw their labor-power simultaneously, he has hold of something, a valuable implement. At the least it can gain for him the rudimentary rights of being able to protest against the killing pace of the "speed-up" without being instantly fired for "inefficiency," "clowning," or "stopping the line."

In the building trades it has been to date a different story, although, with the development of prefabricated materials, the ending may be the same within a few years. At present, however, despite the replacement of the hod by the automatic hoist, and the pick by the pneumatic drill, hand labor, really tool labor, is still important. So are skills and the three to four years of apprenticeship spent to acquire them. Here the worker's bargaining strength depends upon his possession of a comparatively rare facility of hand and eye. He and others in his union have a corner on it, a monopoly, if you choose. And either you buy that particular kind of skill from them or you aren't likely to get it; or if you do, you stand a good chance of going broke, what with the high costs and butter-fingers and general incompetence of strikebreakers.

Moreover, the building-trades worker is far less subordinated to the inexorable routines of the machine than is the mass-production employee. Building construction, by its very nature, is refractory and unpredictable. It is still the temperamental prima donna in the grand opera of American industry. "Even if you build a dog-house," once lamented Stanford White, "you find you have to make it larger because the dog's tail has grown."

The building-trades craftsman is also constantly called on to meet emergencies not foreseen by the best blueprint. He has to exercise his own judgment, out of a knowledge polished by experience. And although it may soon be possible to apply some assembly-line techniques to building method, it is still difficult to envision just how substitutes can be devised for the ingenuity and initiative of the human mind directed to a problem which is generally the same but is specifically always new and different.

When Paul Starrett, contractor extraordinary, was putting up the Empire State Building at the incredibly fast rate of a story a day, he came closer than anyone else perhaps to the assembly-line system in the sense of fitting together standard parts with great speed and precision. At quarry and mill materials had been prepared in advance to facilitate all possible short cuts. Small cranes—operated from ceiling monorails—lifted crates of stone from the trucks, eliminating the usual slower derrick. A cafeteria built and constantly "moved" from the first to the third to the ninth to the twenty-third to the sixty-fourth floor saved thousands of noon-time man hours by providing a good, cheap, and easily accessible eating-place for an army of workers. Yet despite all this emulation of mass-production ways and means, Mr. Starrett still needed 3,500 men of fifty distinctly recognizable skills and organized into nineteen different unions to achieve the almost miraculous efficiency which marked the erection of the world's biggest skyscraper.

In the light of these disciplines and dynamics of the building industry, notably its 78-per-cent need for skilled labor, it is interesting to observe the CIO's recent invasion of this territory, historical stronghold of the AFL, through the medium of the United Construction Workers Organizing Committee. Formed on an industrial basis in August 1939, and directed by A. D. Lewis, John L. Lewis's brother, the UCWOC has put forth the partially valid claim that several tasks can be performed by a single worker, who is therefore "not out of a job when a particular operation stops." In erecting an apartment house, for example, a carpenter might conceivably do the work of a metal-lather, or in sand-hogging a tunnel a drill-runner might turn to form-building. While such practices should assist in maintaining steadier employment, and in banishing jurisdictional squabbles,[1] labor for the construction industry still remains basically a question of the interlocking of various skills. It would after all take a modern Archimedes to be an electrician, a plumber, a hod-carrier, and an expert in elevator cables at one and the same time.

Hence the CIO's entrance into the building-trades field merely confirms the second and significant conclusion that emerges from any objective scrutiny of union forms and functions: namely, that in terms of underlying structure the AFL and the CIO are daily growing more and more alike; and that the whole craft-versus-industrial argument, as explaining the continued division in the American labor movement, has now outlived its cause.

[1] In response to the CIO program, which stresses the abolition of jurisdictional strikes, the AFL Building Trades Department in October 1939 likewise moved to get rid of this traditional plague among its member unions by a policy of "no inter-union strike" agreements with contractors for the duration of a job.

CHAPTER IV

"LIKE FATHER, LIKE SON . . ."

SINCE THE structure of both AFL and CIO has become essentially the same, does their continued warfare result from opposing aims and objectives? The answer is quite emphatically "No." There are differences, to be sure, some of them spectacular; but they are differences in degree, not in kind.

Of course, according to John P. Frey, AFL theologist, the CIO is but a modern version of (1) the Knights of Labor, (2) the Socialist Trades and Labor Alliance, and (3) the I.W.W.'s One Big Union, and is therefore fated to suffer the same failures that marked these three ventures into American labor organization. Although this school of thought has gained an amazingly wide acceptance, even among some ivory-tower students of the labor movement, it is nonsense, from first to last.

It is majestic nonsense, certainly, all fancied up with alleged historical parallelisms. Yet it is based on the kind of logic by which you can prove that (a) since Washington, D. C., national capital of the United States, has a fire department, and since (b) Berlin, Germany's national capital, has a fire department, (c) Washington is ruled by the Nazis. Q.E.D.

In the first place the Noble Order of the Knights of Labor was mainly a reform movement, more political and educational than "unionist." Among its chief attractions were its social-club facilities in a day when cheap cars, movies, and the radio were non-existent. Its greatest leader, Terence V. Powderly, who was at its helm for fourteen years, was less an administrator than an agitator, less a personality than a palpitant preacher of a better day to come. The Order's membership adored his sonorous abstractions, his variations on such themes as "abolition of the wages system," "justice," and "an injury to one is the concern of all," which became the official Knights of Labor slogan. Its intentions were always honorable, and often inspiring. And by means of the elaborate ritualism of its meetings, its flummery of a Masonic initiation raised to the nth power, it did bring a much needed, if momentary, sense of importance, of fraternity, even of anchorage to people bewildered by the shocks and dislocations of the country's rumbling transition from an agrarian to an industrialized economy.

78

To a large extent the Order was a semi-religious crusade, but with fifty-seven different varieties of the Holy Grail. It favored wider distribution of free lands. It was against the money-power, denouncing in a rare flash of realism its stranglehold over credit and currency. It exalted the concept of self-employment by means of a vague Producers Co-operative Commonwealth, which it talked to death. It supported virtually all the panaceas that aimed to make every man a capitalist, even a small one, and in this was thoroughly American; but it formulated no coherent policy for attaining any such result. In 1879, ten years after its founding, every local or branch, called an "assembly," was instructed to devote a certain number of hours per meeting to discussion of "How can the toiler receive a just share of the wealth he creates?" But since the Order's directorate neglected to base such explorations upon any system of labor education, they merely turned attention away from the mundane problem of how to get an extra dollar a week in the pay envelope and transferred it to the supernal plane of pet economic theories while Populists, single-taxers, socialists, free traders, high-tariffers, and Holy Rollers shouted one another down, banging beer mugs on the table with a vehemence that no gavel could subdue.

And to its mixture of ideas the Knights added an equal mixture of people. After 1881 it admitted employers, physicians, and other members of the professions, who intensified its polyglot debating-society character. It excluded, in fact, only gamblers, bankers, procurers, stockbrokers, whisky-distillers, and lawyers, fearing moral leprosy.

In short, its underlying idea was strong and beautiful and eternally appealing: the Brotherhood of Man, no less. But its grasp of the practical economic situation was in inverse ratio to its naïve confused faith in oral millennia.

The rank and file, of course, often showed signs of impatience and grew tired of waiting for Lefty as well as for the new City of the Sun. "They say," complained the Order's secretary, with a note of surprise, "that while our Order deals with measures for the future emancipation of labor, the present necessities should also be considered. . . . The number of men seems very few who . . . can patiently wait until time brings fulfillment of their hopes."

Under pressure from below the Knights did engage in quite a number of successful strikes, notably against Jay Gould's Southern Missouri and Wabash railroads and in many others in the year of the "Great Upheaval," 1886, when it reached a peak of 700,000 members. Many thousands of these newer recruits were drawn from the recent unskilled immigrants, linking language barriers to the Order's already heterogeneous structure and further impeding cohesive action. Then, too, the Knights' program was too remote and highfalutin to hold them and others very long, giving them visions, but no butter for their bread. And by 1895 the Order was for all practical purposes a corpse, although its funeral was officially postponed for another twenty years.

During its long decline, however, the Knights of Labor was nearly captured by a foeman who assailed as infantile its efforts to restore the freer competition of pre-Civil-War days and to create a capitalism which would give everybody an opportunity to be his own boss, and who wanted to turn the Order into something entirely different from what it was. He was Daniel De Leon, born of Spanish-Jewish ancestry on the island of Curaçao, off the coast of Venezuela in December 1852. He was educated in Germany and in New York City, where at Columbia University he took prizes in both constitutional and international law. From his side-forays into economics he decided that he was chosen to play the role of Mohammed to the Allah of Karl Marx. With *Das Kapital* as Koran and Manhattan's lower East Side as Mecca, he began in the mid 1880's, to rescue the American labor movement first from the ignorance and vacuity of the Knights, then from what he derided as the "pure and simple-dom" program of the rising American Federation of Labor with its emphasis upon better wages and shorter hours, here and now.

Domineering, handsome, a "Mephisto with a black

beard," aristocratic in bearing and appearance, he flaunted his polysyllables in order to dazzle the foreign-born workers of German, Irish, and Jewish extraction in the metropolitan area. He attracted to him the genial, quick-witted Patrick J. Murphy, who had "swallowed the Blarney stone" and who was able to make majorities for De Leon, enabling him to dominate the New York City Assembly 49, most important affiliate of the Knights in 1893. Together with J. R. Sovereign, the Populist, De Leon succeeded in ousting Powderly as Grand Master Workman, putting Sovereign in his place. Meanwhile De Leon was enthralling Murphy and others by his depiction of the "new unionist" who "has his heart aflame and his mind inspired with the loftiest thoughts and aspirations." No mean "groveling" improvements or hunger-aggravating crumbs for him. His voice is the clarion's voice: "You are robbed, wealth producers," he cries to the proletariat lying prone; "arouse yourselves; strike off the chains that fetter you as wage slaves; a world of freedom and enjoyment lies ready at your hand; take it . . . leave to your descendents the heritage of . . . Freedom."

And as a sad contrast to this new unionist as envisioned by De Leon, there was that dunderhead AFL member who in following the canny, pragmatic Gompers, "grants the principle of private ownership in the means of production . . . talks about fair and legitimate profits . . . is satisfied with wages . . . has no inkling of the fact that all wealth comes from labor; that all profit . . . is illegitimate and a theft . . . that capital is accumulated profits; or thefts from the workers; that the system under which wages and profits exist is one that tends to increase the latter and reduce the former."

As one of the ruling triumvirate of the Socialist Labor Party, which he had joined in 1890 after a flirtation with Edward Bellamy's Nationalists, De Leon insisted on swinging the Knights from a reform to a revolutionary program. And he might have done it, what with his rhetoric and the expert manipulations of Murphy, who brought the born politician's guile to serve the man whom he thought to be the smartest of his day. But De Leon was in too much of a hurry; he was too impatient and unconciliatory for the tradings of this kind of politics. In a quarrel over policy with J. R. Sovereign, De Leon withdrew his 13,000 members of Assembly 49, giving the disintegrating Knights another push toward its grave. Meantime, while trying to obtain the driver's seat in the Knights with his right hand, he was berating the AFL with his left.

"The dry-rot has set in the American Federation of Labor," he declared in an editorial in the *People*, the Socialist Labor Party organ which he edited. "As an organization [it] is at best a cross between a windbag and a rope of sand; it has no cohesion, vitality or vigor worth mentioning. . . ." And presumably to supply these missing attributes to American labor organization, on a national scale, he urged his devotees who had followed him out of the Knights to "reorganize upon that higher plane . . . of economic and political efforts, consolidated, inspired, guided and purified by the class consciousness of the wage slave." It was this reorganization on a higher plane that was embodied in the Socialist Trades and Labor Alliance, which De Leon next set up to be the new all-inclusive federation of labor of America. He obtained for his Alliance (which from start to finish was a one-man show, his own), the blanket endorsement of the Socialist Labor Party through the following resolution:

Whereas, Both the American Federation of Labor and the Knights of Labor, or what is left of them, have fallen hopelessly into the hands of dishonest and ignorant leaders;

Whereas, these bodies have taken shape as the buffers of capitalism, against whom every intelligent effort of the working class has hitherto gone to pieces;

Whereas, No organization of labor can accomplish anything for the workers that does not proceed from the principle that an irrepressible conflict rages between the capitalist and the working class, a conflict that can be settled only by the total overthrow of the former and the establishment of the Socialist Commonwealth; and

Whereas, This conflict is essentially a political one, needing the combined political and economic efforts of the working class; therefore, be it

Resolved, That we hail with unqualified joy the formation of the Socialist Trade and Labor Alliance as a giant stride towards throwing the yoke of wage slavery and of the robber class the capitalists. We call upon the socialists of the land to carry the revolutionary spirit of the Socialist Trade and Labor Alliance into all the organizations of the workers, and thus consolidate and concentrate the proletariat of America in one irresistible class-conscious army, equipped with both the shield of the economic organization and the sword of the Socialist Labor Party ballot.[1]

However, the hundred-odd unions affiliated with the Alliance were composed primarily of fairly recent immigrants in Manhattan, Brooklyn, and Newark. They had come from countries where sharp class distinctions dominated life. In their campaigns to convert workers from within the AFL as well as from outside, they never made allowance for that ingrained "I'm as good as the next guy" characteristic of American psychology.

Like every Marxist-inspired sect in this country, from the 1850's forward, the Alliance was racked by internal squabbles and doctrinal hair-splittings between the orthodox and the reformers, between the moderate and the merely mad, and soon splinter groups were detaching themselves with all the dissonances of dissolution.

In 1898, with his dream of heading an effective new labor movement, daily vanishing, De Leon essayed a peculiarly clumsy bluff. He issued 228 new charters within six months, but actually to individuals whose

[1] This resolution is not quoted in full.

85

"organizations" wouldn't have filled a single table at a Second Avenue coffee house. When this scheme fizzled, he resorted to sheer invective, that first refuge of a man who is unsure of his course but dare not admit his doubts, even to himself. His opponents within and without the Alliance were branded as "monkeys in convulsions," as "crafty, cold-blooded Judases," and as "crooks, villains and semi-lunatics." And when Phineas T. Barnum joined the dust of the ages, De Leon remarked that for people who had admired the "Great American Humbug" the only consolation to be had was that the perfect substitute, Samuel Gompers, "is still alive."

But all this barbed phrasing, while it lashed Gompers, who detested De Leon, into a frenzy of retaliation in kind, into saying "No more sinister force ever appeared among the socialists," merely underscored the futility of what De Leon and his Alliance represented. Both were exotics. They had no real points of contact, no common meeting-ground with the "average" American worker. They operated always on the fringes and never at the center of the organized labor movement. And they influenced it only to the extent of deepening that distrust of "intellectuals" and "theoreticians" that was already a byword among AFL leaders.

Yet a few years later the always sanguine De Leon, who was determined to be at the head of something, tried again. He planned to gain control over the I.W.W.

—the Industrial Workers of the World—a revolutionary, "direct-action" movement. It combined French syndicalism, Russian anarchism, and English ca' canny with overtones of Socialism, the whole implemented by the rough-neck tactics and violence of the American frontier tradition, especially in the Middle and Far West.

When it was founded in Chicago in 1905, its sponsors were even more varied than its pot-pourri of principles, and were united only by their common hatred of the capitalist system and their desire for its speedy abolition. On the one hand there was William Dudley (Big Bill) Haywood, the moving spirit of the tough Western Federation of Miners, a blunt brawling, bruising, boozing giant of a man, a "bundle of primitive instincts," said Ramsay MacDonald, "a torch amongst a crowd of workers." On the other hand, at the beginning, was Eugene Victor Debs, lean, gentle, a "dedicated" man, of whom James Whitcomb Riley wrote:

And there's Gene Debs—a man 'at stands
And jest holds out in his two hands
As warm a heart as ever beat
Betwixt here and the judgment seat!

In theory an organization in which the individual was to submerge himself utterly in the cause, the I.W.W. soon became a collection of captains who comprised labor's most spectacular ultra-individualists, from the bomb-and-buckshot pamphleteer W. G. Trautman to the so-called "Labor's Joan of Arc," Elizabeth Gurley Flynn, now a Communist, and from the poet Arturo Giovannitti to the militant madonna Mother Jones.

From the outset quarrels over strategy tended to scatter these and other stellar performers to the four winds of doctrine, although frequently—as in the famous Lawrence textile strike in 1912—most of them managed to pull in harness. Meantime, however, the De Leon group, which had captured control for a time and, like the present-day Communists, found that they had merely surrounded themselves, was being edged out by a new element, the "Wobblies." It represented the bundle-stiffs, the migrant workers in grain and fruit fields, the lumberjacks and dock-wallopers, with the more stable gold, silver, and copper miners, and a sprinkling of railroad, brewery, and other workers who felt themselves too hard-boiled and too radical for the AFL. They had guts, and they raised hell and called it holy. They were the most efficient rough-and-tumble gouge-out-his-eye fighters in the United States. They tackled and licked coal and iron police, sheriffs' deputies, and the state militia, using guns, knives, brass knuckles; and they were adept in hitting any particular bull's-eye with a stick of dynamite. They helped workers in forty-one states to win strikes, to preserve rights of free speech and freedom of assembly. Yet the I.W.W. scorned collective-bargaining pacts with employers, save only as a temporary expedient pending the day of the "General Strike," when all workers were somehow to tie up all business activity in knots and then "take over" not only the state's apparatus, from village to federal government, but also the direction of the nation's economic functions as well.

Quite often the I.W.W. called strikes largely to keep the workers "stirred up" and were almost as pleased by defeat as by victory, since the former embittered the "wage-slave" all the more and made him ever more anxious for the "overthrow of capitalism." In the firm belief that "the working class and the employing class have nothing in common," the I.W.W. treated the AFL slogan of a "fair day's pay for a fair day's work" as the invention of "labor fakers" who had sold out to the bosses.

Colorful, often heroic, always turbulent, the I.W.W. by an over-insistence upon "democracy" in its internal affairs decentralized itself to impotency. Its six national departments—mines, manufacturing, agriculture, public service, construction, transportation—existed only on paper. Its rank and file mistrusted unified direction as placing too much power and temptation in the hands of those at the top, and abolished the office of president in 1909. But all this in turn prevented any effective discipline, and helped to keep

89

the I.W.W. more of a guerrilla band than that new "invincible labor army" which at its 1910 height of 100,-000 members it had hoped, in its own phrase, to become. And this lack of centralized authority, along with its basically despairing and pessimistic creed, which repelled rather than attracted most workers, made it possible for the radical baiting saturnalia in the early 1920's to administer a *coup de grâce*, until today the I.W.W. has less than 3,000 members.

Now, it is true, of course, that in one way or another the Knights of Labor, the Socialist Trades and Labor Alliance, and the Industrial Workers of the World were all rivals of the AFL and "dual" to it. And it is also true that both the Alliance and the I.W.W. favored the principle of industrial unionism as a method of increasing "class solidarity." But for Mr. Frey or anyone else to invoke these facts as "proof" that the CIO is the descendant of all three organizations is not only to mistake shadow for substance, but to deny paternity itself. The CIO is no Minerva springing full blown from the head of some strange labor Jove. It is simply the offspring, in direct line, of its parent, the AFL, and bears all the earmarks of this ancestry.

II

THE "like father, like son" resemblance between the AFL and the CIO are more than a metaphor, and go deeper than most people realize. The seven unions which formed the first CIO were among the most efficient, respected and powerful in the Federation. Besides, this first strength of the CIO was soon amplified by still further defections from the AFL when the American Newspaper Guild, the International Furriers Union, the Maritime Union, and nine others switched over from the AFL to the CIO. From John L. Lewis, who for five years in his early career had been Special Field and Legislative Representative for the AFL, peddling the wares of its unionism in coal, copper, steel, and rubber, down to the head of the smallest secessionist local, the leaders [1] of the first CIO had been trained and developed and had learned their jobs within AFL unions. The fact is that the CIO has kept going, and survived employer and AFL opposition and the ravages of recession, because its founders, while active within the Federation for most of their lives, discovered what it takes to build and enlarge unions that can last. What they did was to modernize, to streamline, the same basic strategy that enabled the AFL to become the first labor movement in American history to hold together for more than a dozen years at a time. And that is precisely why the CIO is inherently equipped to establish itself as a permanent rival to the AFL. In theory, merely as competitors, battling in a vacuum, neither

[1] With the exception of Sidney Hillman, who with his Amalgamated Clothing Workers has been in and out of the AFL.

91

side could deliver a knock-out blow to the other, but the practical social and economic results of their conflict are preparing the way for some Joe Louis of reaction to batter them both to a pulp. It is their warfare, and not their philosophy and purpose, that is a menace to American democracy.

Both seek to move and have their beings within the framework of capitalism, the private ownership of the means of production and distribution. Both want that system modified to release our marvelous capacity to create real wealth, goods like bread and shoes, and services like electric light and medical care, from the institutional lags which now prevent the fuller realization of this potentiality.

Both exist primarily to achieve and preserve collective-bargaining agreements between management and unions. Both look upon such agreements not only as a step toward greater union-management co-operation but also as leading toward a time when labor will have a more genuine voice in the conduct of industry—an industrial franchise similar in spirit to the political franchise, the right to vote. Both stress round-table conferences and negotiations with employers as the most sensible and effective way of settling differences over wages, hours and work-conditions. Both regard strikes as a last resort, as a course to be pursued only after all others have failed. Both consider the wage- or salary-earner not as a class-conscious helot, but as a middle-class-conscious American having the same aims and aspirations that animate the rest of the population. Both believe that the stake in the job is quite as much of a property right as a piece of paper signifying ownership of a plant. Both are convinced that as an American the wage- or salary-earner is entitled to some of the good things of life—namely, the opportunity to obtain a job that will provide the comforts available at an income level of $2,500 a year per family, that holds forth some chance of advancement and the putting aside of enough to educate children and to give the worker a little ease and security when old age comes.

Over and above these obvious objectives, common to both the AFL and the CIO, there now appear the first outlines of something else that, in the long run, may transcend all other issues in importance. It is that during the past few years both have been moving, or have been swept, toward a new economic outlook that would place the accent upon a national rather than upon a local, sectional, group, or class approach to remedying the sicknesses of our system. In this respect both the AFL and the CIO are weighing the desirability of trying to achieve an "economy of abundance" by means of a national planning safeguarded by democratic controls.

Both AFL and CIO proponents of this possible "way out" of our present dilemma point to the War Industries Board of 1917–18 and ask, in effect, if we can plan for death and destruction, what is to prevent our planning for peace and prosperity? They contend that unemployment and insecurity are more virulent foes of the democratic way of life than any foreign enemy or any totalitarian gospel. They affirm that planning is an engineering technique and is thus politically non-partisan; that it can be made to serve the aims of democracy quite as easily as it has been debased to serve the ambitions of autarchy's autocracy. They tend to look upon the ill-fated, lop-sided NRA as a first crude groping, foreshadowing of a new and necessary co-ordination between industry, labor, agriculture, and government that will enable the capitalist system to adapt itself more flexibly and more responsively to the needs of a complex, interdependent civilization.

Back in 1935 Matthew Woll, one of the AFL's most representative spokesmen and its most intelligent exemplar of the Gompers pragmatism, indicated this then incipient trend in labor thought. "We will not," he declared, "go back . . . to unbridled, uncontrolled individualism.

"It is true," he continued, "that we as a people and as a nation have before us boundless opportunities for further development. There is no lack of raw materials, whether mineral, textile or foodstuffs, nor of mechanical equipment, capital or human skill. . . . The leadership in this task of rationalizing America's resources cannot come from one man or any particular group of men. It must come from the efficient elements of intelligence in every field and quarter." He added that as a start in this general direction an "Industrial Congress" should be convoked and "be free from State domination, but operate under its beneficent fold."

During the next four years the research and statistical staff of the AFL devoted bulletin after bulletin to the exploration and development of Mr. Woll's thesis until in the June 30, 1939 issue of the Federation's excellent and official *Monthly Survey of Business* it was somewhat telegraphically urged that "sound recovery can only come through planning to advance all economic groups and timing undertakings to provide consuming power to buy output."

Similarly, John L. Lewis and Sidney Hillman, who more than any others shape CIO policy, are perhaps the most ardent advocates of planning to be found in labor circles. As early as October 1931 Hillman was urging the establishment of a National Economic Council to represent the "industrial, financial, transportation, agricultural and labor interests in the United States," to study, and then formulate possible solutions for, pressing economic problems. In the course of Senate hearings on this proposal, Hillman was asked if he agreed that "trade associations within individual industries can achieve the stabilization of the industries." He replied: "Not only do I disagree, but I believe that is not feasible from the whole recorded experience of in-

95

dustry . . . it is impossible for any industry to meet its own problems, apart from other industries. . . . In clothing . . . we have been putting into effect methods to bring about stabilization. We have gone beyond other industries in putting up employment reserves and exchanges. These have helped greatly in normal times," but even then "we did not succeed in achieving complete and real stabilization. . . .

"No one industry can stabilize itself," he continued. "Its prosperity is dependent upon the general state of industry and agriculture. The problem confronting us today is to find jobs for people out of work and to maintain a standard of living to match our productive capacity. We cannot possibly achieve this through planlessness which in the very nature of things must again lead to chaos.

"As I view it," he added, "the fundamental trouble is lack of planning. Assuming that we would go ahead in the province of construction, suppose we should try to erect a building such as the Empire State, over 100 stories high, and use the same engineering that we would use in putting up a barn on a farm, what would happen? . . . It would topple over. . . .

"Assuming that all the industries should inaugurate employment reserves, which I believe in, it would not have any real effect outside of helping a little, unless we come down to the question of planning. We know that we have a population of so many; we have capacity to

96

produce things on a certain scale; and we should run industry accordingly. I do not believe that this would take anything away from our individual theory of running industry, any more than traffic regulation takes away from our individual initiative. Anyone who wants to cross Forty-second street and Broadway with no regard for traffic regulations will soon find no particular use for individual or any other initiative. . . .

"Unless we get planning," he went on, "we are bound to have these depressions; and I certainly do not at all share the point of view of some people who accept these things as inevitable, who say they have always been so and always will continue so. That is a theory of despair. It is the same kind of theory that was held centuries ago, when they had plagues. I can visualize . . . some of the representative citizens saying when the plague broke out, 'Well, nothing can be done. It is an act of God. He will just have a third of the population carried off, and in another ten or twenty years we will make it up, and wait for the next plague.' . . . The surest road to a dictatorship is just not attending to things that have to be done, or at least not finding out what has to be done. . . ."

From his costly experience with the cut-throat competition in the coal industry, and from the early days of the NRA to the present, John L. Lewis has repeatedly asserted that "better living standards cannot be hoped for unless legislative or other provision be made for

97

economic planning and for price, production and profit controls."

At its first Constitutional Convention, in November 1938, the CIO stated as its credo: "It is becoming obvious that full production in a stable economy can be created only by intelligent direction which has the power and the will to co-ordinate all economic controls towards that single end." And in January 1940, speaking before the fiftieth-anniversary convention of his own United Mine Workers, Lewis, in accents curiously reminiscent of Woll's plea of five years before, asked for an immediate national conference between industry, agriculture, labor, and government to lay the groundwork for a concerted attack upon unemployment, and its causes.

Meantime W. Jett Lauck, economic adviser to the United Mine Workers, was busy expanding the American Association for Economic Freedom, which with the co-operation of William Allen White and other liberals was organized in 1938 to proselytize for democratic planning as the next and necessary step in the process of America's economic evolution.

In any event, even in the somewhat ethereal spaces of economic theory, the AFL and the CIO are speaking much the same language. There are, however, certain differences in diction. Toward the whole issue of "planning," for example, about half of the AFL leaders are likely to be lukewarm, indifferent, "resolution-minded." That is, they may pass a resolution approving the general concept "in principle," recommend further investigation, and then forget it. They pride themselves on being "practical" men. They take this to mean that they shouldn't concern themselves overmuch with the larger economic issues. Yet there is a growing socially conscious bloc, led by William Green, George Harrison, and David Dubinsky and supported by such up-and-coming younger men as Harry Van Arsdale, Jr., business agent for the Electrical Workers' largest local, No. 3, which favors the planning idea and is willing to fight for it. Many of the AFL chieftains, of course, remain in doubt about the advantages of relinquishing what in their opinion is the tried and true merit of the old "voluntarism." While they endorsed the Social Security Act and similar measures, they did so reluctantly, warily, with the attitude of "Well, it's a good thing, we guess, so we'd better string along." Many of them expressed the fear that laws of this kind portended too much government intervention and would deprive people of their self-reliance.

All of the CIO leaders, on the other hand, not only cheered the passage of the Social Security Act but also called for more, infinitely more, of the kind of legislation it symbolized. On the whole they believe that more rather than less government "interference" is required to give labor and the common man any kind of chance, to eliminate unemployment, to curb the abuses, the rigidities and excesses of giant corporations; and to a man they welcome national planning as a medium by which the vast economic power now wielded by the few can be canalized into channels of greater social usefulness.

From its inception the CIO has displayed a keener awareness of the potential advantages and the hazards of giving up "voluntarism" than did the AFL. The CIO theorists argued that, once government had been invited to become a partner in promoting the cause of unionism, it stood to reason that you had to try to keep the government on your side lest the very legislative benefits that helped today would be turned into a boomerang tomorrow. Moreover, as previously indicated, the CIO was strongest in the great basic mass-production industries which are national in scope, and markets; and their exercise of social power can be effectively curbed or redirected only by the national rather than state or city governments. The CIO therefore tends to think more in terms of the price and productions controls embodied in the Bituminous Coal Commission, set up by federal enactment to stabilize the anarchic profits and wages condition of the soft-coal industry. The AFL tends to think more in terms of a friendly city administration that will grant building permits only to firms hiring union labor.

Yet both AFL and CIO supported the Fair Labor Standards Act, and both at the moment are co-operating with the United State Housing Authority to remove any possible restraints, on labor's part, to the immediate inauguration of a large-scale slum clearance and small-home-building program. The AFL for example has signed no-strike agreements with the Authority and has created machinery to prevent any jurisdictional rows among its member unions that might delay the completion of any federal project. The CIO has broached plans whereby its construction workers would be employed to put up dwellings, single or multiple, for CIO members in various sections of the country. Hence once more in practice the differences between the Federation and the Congress are far less than their official utterances would seem to imply.

And until early 1940 this has been equally true in the realm of political action itself. To be sure, in the attempt to find a more responsive and efficient agency for reaching its political objectives than that provided by either major party, the CIO in 1936 formed Labor's Non-Partisan League. It sent organizers throughout the country to break the ground for city and state political units that could be later combined into a wide network—perhaps a national "labor-liberal" party for 1940 or 1944. All this was supposed to be contrary to the AFL's traditional non-partisan policy of "Reward your friends, punish your enemies," by voting for Republican or Democratic or other candidates who could show a pro-labor record or who at the least made pro-labor promises. Curiously enough, however, both the League and its one notably successful affiliate, the American Labor Party, turned out to be, at least until 1940, merely technical devices for accomplishing the AFL's historical purpose of rewarding friends and punishing enemies.

The League itself stressed the point that in 1936 it was supporting not the Democratic Party per se, but rather labor's "great and good" friend Franklin Delano Roosevelt. And up until the end of 1939 the League was virtually nothing more than a pressure group tied to the New Deal kite in New York, Pennsylvania, Michigan, Connecticut, New Jersey, and elsewhere.

III

THE New Deal Administration, which by encouraging labor organization in general, unwittingly paved the way for the AFL-CIO split, has been acutely anxious for labor unity and its political effects. The New Deal, after all, in the public's opinion is definitely pro-labor; and anything that labor does adds its bit to the important intangibles which go to make up the voter's mind. Since the AFL-CIO dispute is the most unpopular exhibition in the country today, practical politicians fear that the feelings of resentment it has aroused would be, by process of transference, carried over to the New Deal itself. But there have been less subtle rea-

102

sons for White House pressure to promote AFL-CIO accord, a pressure that has increased in resourcefulness and intensity over the past two years, but to no avail.

New Dealers remember that in 1936 Pennsylvania was captured for Roosevelt primarily because the AFL and the CIO, despite their differences, stood together politically behind the most brilliant publicity campaign in labor annals. In 1938, however, the AFL went officially Republican in the Keystone State in order to injure the CIO, which was busy with its own adventures on the fringes of the state's Democratic Party; with the result that the G.O.P. scored a resounding victory, with all it meant in terms of patronage, prestige, and election machinery for 1940. Naturally, White House advisers were alarmed lest this same kind of performance be repeated on a national scale.

While it remains true that the AFL vote in presidential contests has never been "deliverable" in the Tammany ward-heeler's use of the word, enough of it can be "directed," state by state, to win or lose national elections, especially in a close year. Hence the risk, as New Dealers saw it, that if the feud between the AFL and the CIO continued, a good share of the AFL's ballot strength would go to the Republicans— unless they nominated an out-and-out reactionary.

The proof that G.O.P. leaders were already looking in this direction appeared at the AFL 1939 convention when Frank Duffy, first vice-president of the Executive Council and secretary of the Carpenters, startled the delegates by first resigning and then placing in nomination his boss—and Edgar Bergen—Big Bill Hutcheson, head of the Carpenters. Hutcheson is chairman of the Republican Labor Committee and had been assured the post of Secretary of Labor in the event of a Republican victory in 1940. His return to personal participation in the affairs of the council was simply to head off the New Deal support being drummed up by Dan Tobin and William Green and to prevent any thoroughgoing AFL endorsement, even indirectly, of the Roosevelt administration. Hutcheson had fertile soil in which to work. The AFL rank and file were still smarting under the administration's attitude toward maintaining wage-scales on WPA projects and toward "striking against the government." Nor does the AFL as a whole like the administration's fondness for the military mind in alphabetical-agency positions. And the Federation's reaction to M-Day plans as now formulated, and to Thurman Arnold's use of the Sherman Anti-Trust Law to indict unions in the building industry on grounds of conspiracy in restraint of trade, has been at once angry and suspicious. By and large, however, this kind of antagonism has been canceled out; the average AFL member and his officers think that the New Deal labor record, with all its faults, is something to be upheld, and it will be supported by "unofficial" persuasions and pronouncements for some time to come.

There is, of course, a considerable school of opinion within the AFL that adheres strictly to the Gompers doctrine of dividing up the AFL's political support by atomizing it, by selecting a candidate here and rejecting another there, as individuals, on the basis of their labor chevrons irrespective of party labels, rather than accepting an entire party's labor program. Matthew Woll, for example, has plumped for this point of view, dividing the Federation politically into three parts: the Hutcheson-Republican segment, the Green-Tobin-New-Deal faction, and the Woll "neutral" and "independent" group, Republican, Democratic, and Mugwump.

The CIO, which was generally believed to be far more strongly attached to the New Deal and all its works than the AFL, has been split down the middle by even sharper differences on the question of *Realpolitik*. John L. Lewis, together with the CIO Stalinists, were determined to cut the CIO off from the Democratic Party and to build up Labor's Non-Partisan League as the basis for a national third-party movement, looking ahead to 1944. Lewis embarked upon this course because he had convinced himself that the New Deal was letting labor down; that the Democratic Party, after making some concessions to liberalism, had reverted to type, with its corrupt Northern city machines like Tammany Hall in New York, and the Nash-Kelly camarilla in Chicago, and its reactionary Southern politicos resuming their places in the driver's seat. He also convinced himself that the Democratic Party had no effective solution for unemployment and its kindred ills; and he was eager to restore his own political power, which he had thrown out of the window by openly breaking with Roosevelt early in 1940, predicting Roosevelt's "ignominious defeat" in any third-term bid. The Stalinists favored the third-party adventure because as sympathizers and messenger boys of the Soviet Union they were opposed to the administration's pronounced pro-Ally bias. In addition to stirring up anti-New-Deal views within the CIO, they formed "innocent front" peace organizations such as the Yanks Are Not Coming Committee to proselytize for an "isolationism" quite as rabid as their interventionist pleas prior to the Hitler-Stalin pact.[1]

The Lewis strategy is to use the issues of the 1940 presidential campaign to strengthen Labor's Non-Partisan League and link it with other potential third-party alignments for independent political action, on the basis of dramatizing the needs of the domestic, as against the foreign, front. He perceives, however, that any such third party must rest on plinths wider and

[1] For a more detailed discussion of Stalinists in the CIO see pages 128 et seq., in the next chapter.

106

bigger than those of the unions alone. And to reach out toward this necessary mass base he has been negotiating with leaders in the Townsend Old Age Pension Plan, the American Youth Congress, the National Negro Congress, the Workers' Alliance, and the like, speaking before their meetings and trying to prepare them for future association with his own political party. He proceeds upon the assumption that such grievance groups as the aged, the underprivileged, and the unemployed are mobilized as never before, and that what he has to do is first to capture them and then enlarge them. He is gambling on what in his opinion is the high probability that the disintegrating forces of ten years of depression will persist for yet another four, whichever major party may be in power. He envisions himself as the Warwick, or perhaps the standard-bearer of those who, denied a meed of participation in the economy, will be ready for change—drastic change— especially if it seems to offer the jobs and security which neither Democrats nor Republicans are likely to provide.

At the moment, however, Lewis's primary obstacle is the attitude of the overwhelming majority of the CIO membership, who want to stick with Roosevelt, or whoever will wear his mantle in the next few years. The exemplar of this sentiment is Sidney Hillman, second only to Lewis in CIO councils. Hillman is a devout New Dealer and with great regularity and finesse he has been thwarting Lewis's plans to prevent Labor's Non-Partisan League from endorsing Roosevelt and a third term. In New York State the Hillman influence, together with that of other needle-trades chieftains, maintained control of the American Labor Party, with its pivotal 400,000 or more votes, against the vigorous attempts of a Stalinist faction, encouraged by Lewis, to wrest its direction from the pro-New-Deal and Roosevelt bloc. Similarly in Newark in April 1940 Hillman swung New Jersey's Labor's Non-Partisan League to the support of Roosevelt for a third term by a vote of 177 to 101, despite Lewis's somewhat frantic efforts to prevent what his backers described as "handing a blank check to Roosevelt."

The fly in the Lewis third-party ointment is that New York's American Labor Party and the New Jersey branch of the League are perhaps the two most powerful political arms of the CIO. In Pennsylvania, Michigan, Ohio, Massachusetts, and other industrial centers where the League has established auxiliaries, Lewis has continued to encounter stiff opposition to his third-party aspirations, even among his own United Mine Workers. At present he therefore lacks that priceless ingredient of any third-party movement: firm and well-organized nuclei in various states. And even if Lewis could do some political trading with Philip LaFollette, the latter's National Progressive Association has remained the abortion it has been since its beginnings in

1938. Indeed, LaFollette is having quite as hard a time to revive the Progressive Party in his native Wisconsin alone as the remnants of Floyd Olsen's Farmer-Labor party are having to revitalize their following in Minnesota. The agrarian Non-Partisan League of North Dakota is not what it was in its halcyon days. The Commonwealth Federation in Washington and Oregon is being shattered by internal strife between Communist and non-Communist elements. The residue of the Upton Sinclair EPIC movement in California is likewise in bad shape. In short, third-party potentialities at the moment would seem to be even less propitious than in 1924, when Robert M. LaFollette and Burton K. Wheeler received nearly five million votes on their Progressive-Independent ticket from labor, agricultural, and liberal groups and a Socialist Party relatively far stronger than it is today.

And while the political division within the CIO is yet another point of similarity to the AFL, the former's situation is far more serious in this respect. It may presage an organizational split of a kind that AFL political differences have never provoked. The third-party issue has added fuel to the flame of other disagreements between Lewis and Hillman, the two most influential figures in the CIO.

Until recently they have complemented each other with great effectiveness; they are contrasts ready made for novelist or playwright. Lewis, with his graying mane of mud-colored hair, his great tragic slate-blue eyes, his extravagant brows, his oratorical periods, his squat, supple bull-of-Bashan build, his prognathous jaw, is as theatrical in appearance as in behavior. On the other hand, Hillman, trim, compact, of average height, with thoughtful, dreamy, cobalt eyes and a spatulous nose, is reserved, quiet, even shy. Lewis looks like a Shakespearian actor about to declaim, Hillman like a college professor impatient with trivia not germane to the moment's discussion. Lewis is at once intuitive and abstract, playing his hunches on the grand scale; Hillman is more analytical, moving only after careful calculation of all the particulars; Lewis goes into the ring rushing to land the one-two punch for the knock-out blow; Hillman is an adroit boxer, coldly cutting his opponent down. Lewis is blunt, Hillman diplomatic. Lewis is an extremist, willing to risk greatly on an all-or-nothing basis; Hillman will ask for all, accept less, make it secure, and come back for more later on. Lewis revels in the platform's spotlight, Hillman prefers the exchanges of the conference table.

Hillman is the CIO's most ardent advocate of unity with the AFL and has vigorously opposed the CIO's recent invasion of the building field, stronghold of the Federation. On the other hand, Lewis has refused to resume peace negotiations with the AFL and regards the CIO United Construction Workers, competitor of the Federation's Bricklayers, Plumbers, et cetera, as the apple of his eye. Then, too, Lewis and Hillman are at cross-purposes on timing and tactics. Hillman agrees with Lewis that unemployment is our most crucial, pressing problem. He also agrees with Lewis that a national conference of industry, agriculture, labor, and government, of the kind that Lewis proposed in his speech before the United Mine Workers' fiftieth convention at Columbus in January 1939, is a valuable and necessary step. But Hillman claims that an election year, especially a show-down year such as 1940, is not a strategic time for launching any such undertaking; that labor's first job is to defend and conserve gains already won under the New Deal—gains now vitally menaced. He asserts further that certain Tory interests which would naturally have to participate in the type of national conference suggested by Lewis would attend it right enough, but merely to sabotage it at this time, and for so long as they believe that they have the chance to rout the New Deal and overturn its reforms. It is Hillman's contention that only after the New Deal and its direction have been again vindicated at the polls would such puissant Tory groups in finance and industry be willing to sit down around the table, make concessions, and discuss in earnest some new co-ordination of the American economy that might provide a more efficient and equitable production and distribution of wealth.

Meanwhile, unless Lewis should modify his views

111

toward Roosevelt, the New Deal, and AFL-CIO unity, Hillman and his followers in the Clothing, Textile, Laundry, Retail and Wholesale, Auto and Rubber unions will put on a last-ditch fight to curb what they consider to be Lewis's arbitrary decision to form a third party at this time. And should Hillman and his supporters fail in this effort, it would surprise very few insiders to see him take a walk out of the CIO, carrying at least five among its strongest affiliates with him.

CHAPTER V

STATES' RIGHTS AND NATIONAL GOVERNMENT

MEANWHILE voices from both left and right proclaim that the real difference between the AFL and the CIO is that the former in its own internal government is a democracy while the CIO is a dictatorship.

Both, of course, are bodies of autonomous more or less self-governing unions—the AFL more, the CIO less. The AFL is a "federation" in name and in reality. It is more loosely knit than the CIO, granting to its affiliates wider latitude and self-determination than does its rival. The Federation's component unions may be compared to the American states in the early days of the Republic, say, when John Adams was President, and each sovereign commonwealth, Virginia as well as Massachusetts, was jealous of its own authority and reluctant to relinquish a jot or tittle of it to the national government. "Inherently," said Gompers in 1907, "an

113

international union is sovereign to itself"; and ever since the AFL has carried this "states' rights" doctrine to a Jeffersonian extreme.

The AFL is governed by its annual convention, where the unions are represented on the basis of their dues-paying enrollment. A single delegate is allowed to the individual union for its every four thousand members, or fraction thereof; and each delegate in turn is allowed one vote for each hundred members of his union, which elects him or others annually to participate in the deliberations of the convention, which is at once the Federation's law-making body and its highest tribunal. The AFL also grants a single vote each to its 770 City Centrals, which in their respective communities fuse the Federation's affiliates into a single organization to advance and protect their common interests in vocational training in the schools, municipal legislation, and other problems of local concern. And to each of the AFL's forty-nine state federations, which deal chiefly with labor legislation and educational programs and which are manned by officers chosen by the City Centrals and the unions of whatever kind,[1] is given but a single vote.

It is the Executive Council that is the AFL's administrative branch and that, over the past few years par-

[1] There are also the federal trade locals and the federal labor locals. The first are a craft group directly affiliated with the national AFL since no union exists in its field, and the latter are a catch-all of workers in all occupations who have not yet been assigned their

114

ticularly, has tended to absorb judicial functions as well. At present the balance of power within the council is lodged in such building-trades leaders as Big Bill Hutcheson of the Carpenters and George Meany (secretary-treasurer) of the Plumbers; in G. M. Bugniazet of the Electricians; Harry C. Bates of the Bricklayers, Daniel Tobin of the Teamsters, and Harvey Brown of the Machinists, Matthew Woll of the Photo-Engravers, and George M. Harrison of the Railway Clerks.

The council can make or break AFL presidents, direct the expenditures of funds for organizing-campaigns and for strikes, and by one means or another exert telling pressure upon the selection of delegates from their own and other unions. For they are chosen not upon any basis of proportional representation but rather upon their ability to handle people, their capacity for leadership of a kind that often resembles that of the political boss. Yet in one sense they have to be that way; for the Federation is founded upon the suasions of "moral power" rather than upon any rigid variation of the laws of the Medes and the Persians.

"The affiliated organizations of the American Federation of Labor," wrote Gompers in 1911, "are held together by moral obligation, a spirit of comraderie, a spirit of group patriotism, a spirit of mutual assistance."

---

jurisdictional guardians. Together in 1940 these groups comprised about 300,000 people, who are also permitted to send voting delegates to the convention.

115

And it is for this very reason that the council, convening four times yearly to carry out the mandates of the convention and to manage the AFL's interim affairs, has been often hog-tied by its lack of formal statutes of governance, by the Federation's crusty custom of allowing to its constituent unions a liberty of action that easily degenerates into the anarchy of license.

The council, composed of fifteen vice-presidents elected annually by the convention (plus the president and the secretary-treasurer), has often made rulings to allot jurisdictional territory to one member union as against another only to find that if a strong union didn't like that decision, it was conspicuously ignored. The council is not implemented to compel any affiliate to comply with its edicts. Practically, the council can only invoke oral argument and the common good to bring a nose-thumbing rebel into line. It can, to be sure, suspend an affiliate's charter, but only for (a) non-payment of per capita dues or (b) failure to pay strike assessments.[1] Only the annual convention of the AFL can get down to brass tacks and suspend or expel a recalcitrant union, and then only by a two-thirds majority roll-call vote, a clumsy and unwieldy process that gets the Federation into all kinds of hot water.

During the past thirty-eight years, for example, the Brotherhood of Teamsters and the Brewery Workers

[1] As previously noted, the council's expulsion of the first CIO was a flagrant and utterly illegal assumption of an authority it never possessed.

116

Union have waged unremitting warfare on each other over the dues and allegiance of beer-wagon and truck drivers. In 1933 the council finally awarded this jurisdiction to the Teamsters, instructing the Brewery Workers Union to transfer its 11,400 drivers to the Brotherhood. The Brewery Workers Union refused. It assailed the decision as monstrously unfair and as more of a tribute to the influence of the Teamsters, which with its 400,000 members is the AFL's largest affiliate, than as any excursion into the realm of even-handed justice. The Brewery Workers Union went even further. It sought and obtained an injunction from a District of Columbia federal court that not only restrains the Teamsters from taking over the beer drivers but also challenges the authority of the Federation to settle jurisdictional disputes among its own affiliates. All this came as a soul-shattering surprise to the AFL, since a cardinal tenet of its existence is its right to guarantee control over a certain work area to its affiliates and to act as arbiter when quarrels over this question arise.

In this particular case, however, the Brewery Workers Union has raised a point that has already become a *cause célèbre* in labor circles. "Well, now," argues the BWU in effect, "from the day of our birth fifty-three years ago we have been and remain an industrial union. That means our jurisdiction covers *all* brewery workers, including drivers. When in 1887 we obtained a charter from the American Federation of Labor, that organization, in the very process of letting us affiliate, acknowledged our right to include drivers along with the other workers in our industry. This is especially true since Article 9, Section 11, of the AFL Constitution declares that no charter can be issued to an applicant union 'without a positive and clear definition of the trade jurisdiction claimed.' We defined our jurisdiction as embracing drivers. The AFL accepted us on that basis. We can find nothing in the AFL Constitution that empowers the Executive Council or anyone else to force us to give up our drivers to the Teamsters. We realize that the convention can get rid of us entirely by a two-thirds majority vote, but that is a horse of a different color—and, anyway, there's always the CIO."

For more than half a century the proceedings of AFL conventions abound with still other illustrations of this kind of internecine strife, with the Carpenters heading the list of unions claiming certain work for themselves alone. For twenty-five years, for instance, the Carpenters and Sheet-Metal Workers battled over which one should hang metal doors and lay metal casings or trim. The Carpenters and the Plumbers disputed the right to bore holes in wooden floors for the installation of pipe. The Painters tried to prevent the Electricians from painting fire-alarm and police-"report" boxes and electrical poles. The Stone Cutters and the Granite Cutters both wanted control over artificial

118

stone. The Flint Glass Workers and the Bottle Blowers are at loggerheads today over who gets whom among the workers turning out neon signs. The Butchers claim priority over the Retail Clerks in meat markets.

In seeking to curb or avoid this costly dissension which alienates public sympathy for unionism as much as any single factor, the AFL's policy up to the past year has been merely that of expediency, vacillation, and power politics. In 1924, in the metal-trim squabble, the AFL decided against the Carpenters and for the Sheet-Metal Workers. The former promptly picked up its marbles and sulked home and slammed the door. But the absence of so potent an affiliate, and the financial loss of its refusal to pay any more dues, proved unendurable to the AFL. The case was reopened in 1927 and the decision reversed. The Carpenters returned to the fold, for the regular receipt of their money was considered less fatiguing than the continued exercise of "moral power."

From time to time there have been four different AFL agencies seeking to exorcize this demon of jurisdictional disputes. The Executive Council has remained a constant court in this respect, sitting as a whole or working through an adjustment sub-committee. Then there are the three great AFL departments,[1]

---

[1] The fourth AFL department is that of the Union Label, which, as its name implies, promotes the cause of union-made products among labor and the general public.

building trades, metal trades, and railway employees, which largely owe their origins to jurisdictional conflict and which have respectively settled them with varying success. In 1919 the Federation established a National Board of Jurisdictional Awards, which held high promise during its first years, but lost face and force when in 1927 it gave the Carpenters things previously taken away. During the past four years, and especially since early 1939, the building-trades department, whose member unions had been incessantly embroiled over work rights, formulated a dual program that, at long last, seems to hold out hope that the jitters of jurisdiction in the construction industry will be greatly allayed. Under this formula, local unions are given the chance to iron out their differences by mutual discussion, but with no work stoppage on the job. If disputes cannot be settled locally, the national officers of the opposing union may select an arbitrator who conducts hearings, still without any work stoppage, and whose decisions are "binding and final" upon both sides. Latterly this policy has been extended by a new kind of agreement with contractors under which all AFL unions employed at a particular site guarantee jointly that there will be no cessation of activity as a result of jurisdictional conflicts "for the duration." Although previously debated within the AFL, this step was somewhat suddenly taken in the late summer of 1939 to blunt the appeal of the CIO Construction Workers that by putting all employees in industrial unions the banshee of jurisdictional scrapping would be banished once and for all. And whereas under its new "strikeless" system jurisdictional fights among AFL unions have been declining in number and intensity month by month, this trend may be arrested at any moment by the Federation's inherent lack of final enforcement powers, which makes it still resemble a weak feudal king at the mercy of his bickering barons. For the AFL clings stubbornly to the "autonomy" of its affiliates, inspired in part by its maudlin and muddled devotion to the "good old days," in part by the naturally selfish urgency of each union to control as much work as it can lay hands on, and in part by the personal ambitions, mutual jealousies and rivalries, and even the corruption of various business agents and other chieftains.

At the Federation's 1939 convention, for instance, Delegate Mary E. Rider of the Trades and Labor Union in St. Louis proposed that:

Whereas, Frequent labor disputes have become a menace and detriment to the organized labor movement, resulting in bitter strife in the ranks and serious loss of time to all involved, this applying to jurisdictional disputes; and

Whereas, Such . . . are generally condemned by both the press and the public and our organized labor movement as a nuisance interfering with the rights of others, we believe it about time that some remedy be promptly applied to solve this serious problem; therefore be it

Resolved, That we, the officers and delegates of the

121

Central Trades and Labor Union of St. Louis and Vicinity in meeting assembled this 27th day of August 1939, do hereby respectfully suggest and earnestly request that the next convention of the AFL will take some action by creating the office of High Commissioner or some other adequate means to suppress and eliminate jurisdictional strikes. . . .[1]

But the resolutions committee replied, as its progenitors have been replying for two generations, that while it was "in full accord with the thought that jurisdictional disputes and strikes be avoided until a verdict has been rendered by the proper authority within the AFL," it simply couldn't abide the idea of lodging that authority in "a high commissioner or some other designated group."

Rather, the committee declared, "As the conventions of the American Federation of Labor are the supreme authority to decide questions of jurisdiction, and should remain so, your Committee recommends non-concurrence." And, as usual, that was that.

Despite this evidence of a narrow outmoded approach to inter-union combat, it would be a mistake to assume that industrial unionism would eliminate jurisdictional warfare quite as automatically as CIO spokesmen assert. That the CIO has been so far at least virtually immune from this plague is due less to its emphasis upon form than to the intelligence and imagination of a leadership intent upon building a strong,

[1] Resolution quoted only in part.

122

cohesive organization. Yet certain questions as to jurisdictional boundaries already are coming up. The General Motors Corporation, for instance, has a subsidiary which manufactures the Frigidaire, an electrical mechanism. Should the labor force in Frigidaire plants belong to the CIO United Automobile Workers or to the CIO Radio, Electrical and Machine Workers? When the Goodyear Rubber Company's tire-fabric factory is unionized, should it be done by the United Rubber Workers or by the cotton division of the Textile Workers' Union? It is more than likely that inventive and industrial changes, the use of new materials and methods, may blur many of the lines of demarcation among CIO as well as AFL unions.

In part to sidestep the colossal extravagance of jurisdictional rows, the CIO centralized its own internal government to an extent that would have delighted the soul of Alexander Hamilton. Like the AFL, of course, the "supreme authority" of the CIO is vested in the annual convention. In theory the CIO's Executive Board of forty-four is the counterpart of the AFL's Executive Council. In practice, however, the CIO's six vice-presidents, together with its president and secretary-treasurer, more closely parallel the council's functions.[1] The CIO has its state and city (sometimes county) Indus-

[1] President John L. Lewis of the United Mine Workers; Secretary-Treasurer James B. Carey of the United Radio, Electrical and Machine Workers; vice-presidents Sidney Hillman of the Amalgamated Clothing Workers; Philip Murray of the Steel Workers' Organ-

123

trial Union Councils, which duplicate the AFL's State Federations and City Centrals in every vital respect. However, under the provisions of the CIO Constitution, adopted in November 1938, the president is given the dualistic role of administrator and magistrate. Subject to review by the Executive Board, which convenes twice yearly, he may "interpret the meaning of the constitution" and, subject to the approval of the Executive Board, he may "appoint, direct, suspend, or remove such organizers, representatives, agents, and employees as he may deem necessary." Moreover, the Executive Board is empowered to "file charges and conduct hearings . . . against any officer of the Organization or any member of the Executive Board, on the ground that such person is guilty of malfeasance or maladministration, and to make a report to the convention recommending appropriate action." No such broad disciplinary powers are specifically assigned to the AFL Executive Council. While the AFL leadership cannot intervene in the conduct of an affiliated union, it would seem that the CIO would be able to do so, despite disclaimers that the intent of the "malfeasance" section is confined only to officials in their capacity as CIO office-holders and not as leaders of individual unions.

---

izing Committee; Emil Rieve, Textile Workers' Union; R. J. Thomas, United Automobile Workers; S. H. Dalrymple, United Rubber Workers; Reid Robinson, Mine, Mill and Smelter Workers. All these CIO officers are the heads of their respective unions.

124

On the whole, however, the CIO's greater compactness of control and greater executive authority exist less in its constitution than in its actual working set-up. When early in 1939 John L. Lewis proposed to William Green that, to promote the interests of labor peace and unity, they both resign their posts, Green retorted that if he quit it would deprive the AFL of its present leadership. He added, however, that if Lewis resigned, the actual direction and distribution of power within the CIO would not be changed at all, since Lewis would still exercise genuine control through the United Mine Workers and the unions and organizing committees which depend upon it for sustenance and guidance alike. And this is quite definitely true, of course. The Steel Workers' Organizing Committee is in this sense an appendage of the Miners, and is led by Philip Murray, a vice-president of the Miners, and Lewis's right bower. Of the $1,500,000 spent in the steel organizing-campaign, $1,078,000 was given by the Miners. Likewise the Gas, By-Product Coke and Chemical Workers Union is a subsidiary of the Miners, and for the same reasons. Five other committees and three other unions owe or owed their existence to the Miners, in money and initiating personnel. By the same token the Textile Workers' Organizing Committee, which in May 1939 became a full-fledged union on its own, the Laundry Workers, and the Wholesale and Retail Clerks were all in their beginnings and nursing stages merely extensions of Sidney Hillman's Amalgamated Clothing Workers, from which they received anywhere from $80,000 to more than $800,000 in cash on the line.

Moreover, John L. Lewis draws no salary as president of the CIO, which until its 1939 convention had no paid national officers and then provided only for a full-time secretary-treasurer. But Lewis does draw $25,000 a year as head of the Miners. William Green's salary of $12,000 per annum is paid by the AFL as a whole.

When confronted by this situation, CIO opponents cry out that of course John L. Lewis is dictatorial by nature and he has naturally fashioned the CIO government in his own image, and they also imply that all this intense centralizing of authority reflects the hand of Joseph Stalin and his American agents. Both accusations are partially correct, but they are too often wrenched from their context and assigned an importance they do not deserve. Fundamentally, not Cæsarism but an industrial map of the United States, not Communism but a calendar, explain the excessive lumping of control in the hands of the CIO's top-ranking trio, John L. Lewis, Sidney Hillman, and Philip Murray.

The CIO is young. It is but four and a half years old, but big for its age. Growing fast at the outset, perhaps too fast, it has not yet had time to train and season a sufficient number of executives whose judgment would reflect that rightness which only experience in office and afield can bring. Hence, Lewis, Hillman, and Murray and others of the CIO high command have had to double in brass pending the development of relatively raw recruits, however talented, into aids and associates who can relieve them of their heavy responsibilities. At the moment the CIO's Executive Board itself, representing the cream of the entire membership, contains more lieutenants and captains than division commanders, mainly because in union as in military affairs you simply can't grow first-rate superior officers by hot-house methods.

None of the CIO's ruling triumvirate is any too happy over this situation. They have been compelled during the past few years to live in an atmosphere of perpetual emergency, of constantly backing up the line, of immersing themselves in detail and trouble-shooting to straighten out the snarls of new unions, when all three of them should have been giving their time to the formulation of high strategy. All three have been subjected to the kind of nervous tensions that make men old before their time. Late in 1938, for example, Hillman nearly succumbed to pneumonia, the severity of which was induced directly by the strain and fatigue of sheer overwork.

But the CIO's greater "density of power" as compared with that prevailing within the AFL stems from another, more basic source than the difficulty of making

127

colonels out of corporals in a few short years. It is again simply that the laws of supply and demand which govern the sale of labor energy in the mass-production spheres where the CIO is strongest require a national leadership empowered to act with alacrity and precision on a national scale. That leadership, to enforce union standards over an entire industry like coal with scattered mines, or men's clothing with far-spread factories, or textiles and other realms, must be free and untrammeled and endowed with final authority. It has to deal not with a single employer, locally, but with trade associations representing all or the majority of employers within an industry all over the United States. It must be able to make quick decisions, to call strikes swiftly in Illinois as in Alabama, in Oregon as in Maryland, over perhaps fifty widely separated points. It must be able to issue press releases promptly, summon legal and statistical aid on the run, and be unhindered in its rights to seize a concession in conference-room negotiations. And with the United Mine Workers and the Amalgamated Clothing Workers becoming the prime movers in the CIO, this body has tended naturally to reflect these habits and practices of concentrated leadership which both the Miners and the Clothing Workers have found vital not only to their efficiency but also to their existence.

It happened that the Communists, or more properly the Stalinists, were the chief beneficiaries of this centralizing trend, and they promoted it in every way possible since it dovetailed with their own totalitarian belief in all power to the all highest. By getting a handful of their people into key spots they were able to exert an influence far out of proportion to their numerical strength, to garrotte many rank-and-file uprisings against their iron-handed rule, to cause the defection of such promising unions as the Southern Tenant Farmers from the CIO, to repel thousands of workers who otherwise would have joined the CIO, and to do the CIO a perhaps irreparable amount of harm.

When the CIO in its first manifestations as a Committee started to move forward in high gear in 1936 and 1937, it found many thousands of workers anxious to sign up. It also found itself unexpectedly embroiled on a dozen different fronts at once. It had designed its original strategy to hurl its new might in money and men against Big Steel. It believed that once this stronghold of the open shop had been captured for collective bargaining, it would be easier to move into other salients. But unforeseen events ruined this carefully calculated maneuver. The great spontaneous sit-down of December 1936 to February 1937 in the auto industry dumped a big dramatic strike into the CIO's lap. Then there was trouble in glass, and more trouble in rubber.

Beset on all sides at once, short of trained manpower, Lewis accepted proffers of aid from the Stalinists pretty much in accord with Henry of Navarre's

129

proverb: "In a battle I make arrows from any wood." Lewis was in a tough fight. He needed help. The Stalinists were equipped to supply some of it.

In 1920 the Communist International, through its subsidiary, the Red International Labor Union, ordered all Communist units in seventeen different countries to "establish Communist nuclei" in labor unions, and to capture them for the world revolution "by boring from within." In the United States, shortly thereafter, the Workers (Communist) Party published a translation of Lenin's pamphlet *Should Communists Participate in Reactionary Trade Unions?* The answer was emphatically: "Yes." Moreover, since the end justified the means, party members were advised to "practice trickery, to employ cunning, to resort to illegal methods, to even overlook or conceal the truth." These instructions were taken to heart especially by William Z. Foster, leading Communist of the early 1920's, a former competent organizer for the I.W.W. He transferred his old anarcho-syndicalist Trade Union Educational League, then moribund, to the AFL as a propaganda group that would convert Federation members to an ultimate Communism. As an organizer for the AFL in the 1919 steel campaign he had rendered yeoman service, but his creation of the T.U.E.L., which was attached to the Red International Labor Union, made him suspect and he and his partisans were soon ousted. But his faith in the efficacy of boring from within remained unshaken.

130

In 1923 he denounced "dual unionism," the whole process of setting up rival organizations, as "a malignant disease that sickens and devitalizes the whole labor movement . . . a useless and insupportable squandering of
labor's most precious life force . . . a bottomless pit
into which the workers have vainly thrown their energy
and idealism. . . ." But in 1928 the Red International
Labor Union reversed its former policy of anti-dualism
and commanded the immediate establishment of rival
union centers in the United States, since the AFL was
"non-militant" and was in any case ejecting any Communists or their sympathizers it could find. Hence Foster rechristened his organization the Trade Union Unity
League, which served as a holding company for the
new independent dual unions that the Communist
Party began to fashion. Chief of these was the National
Miners Union, which led several strikes in Ohio, West
Virginia, and Pennsylvania, but made no substantial
inroads upon the United Mine Workers, or upon the
leadership of John L. Lewis, whom the Communists
accused of (1) murder, (2) betraying the miners in
the manner of (a) a Judas, (b) a ruthless machine politician, and (c) a strikebreaker secretly in the pay of the
bosses. The Communist Needle Trades Workers Industrial Union was more "successful," won ascendancy
over the vital Joint Board of Cloakmakers in the International Ladies' Garment Workers Union, and called
an utterly senseless strike which bled this union white

and nearly destroyed it entirely. The third major Communist union was that of the National Textile Workers, which invaded the Southern textile area with class-struggle slogans that hindered the development of any bona-fide unionism, especially in Georgia, North and South Carolina, and Alabama for some years. Altogether the T.U.U.L. and its affiliates, which included many regional [1] and national unions which never emerged from the paper stage, claimed about 57,000 members.

But in 1935 the Trade Union Unity League was formally dissolved in response to new instructions from the Communist International. The Soviet Union, thinking itself threatened in both terms of territory and rival terrorism by the rising tide of German and Japanese Fascism, had embarked upon the so-called "Litvinov policy" of seeking to link its destiny with that of the democracies in international affairs. Promptly in this country as elsewhere Communists turned about face with the precision of a well-disciplined soldiery as the "united front," with reform, liberal, and labor groups,

[1] Some of these largely imaginary organizations were: Auto Workers Union, Building Maintenance Workers Union, Cannery and Agricultural Workers Union, Doll and Toy Workers Union, Food and Packinghouse Industrial Union, Jewelry Workers Industrial Union, Novelty Leather Workers Union, Office Workers Union, Photograph Workers Industrial Union, Steel and Metal Workers Industrial Union, Tobacco Workers Industrial Union, Wholesale Dry Goods Workers Union, and many more.

132

became the new order of the day. Thus Roosevelt, who in 1934 was assailed by the Communist Party press as a social Fascist and a tool of Wall Street, was with aplomb transformed into a pure and stainless knight, the defender of the newly sacred democratic faith. Thus the AFL unions, which in 1934 [1] were corrupt, reactionary devices for selling out labor to the bosses, were in 1935 instruments for the liberation of the working class.

It must be remembered that this change in the party line coincided with the formation of the CIO in November 1935. And while the framework of unions that ramified from the parent T.U.U.L. was being disbanded, their directing personnel was offered to Lewis on a silver platter. He felt he could use, if not their philosophy, at least their experience. For in trying to secure a mass following for the T.U.U.L., they had learned the ropes of union organization. They knew how to make speeches, write reports, run mimeograph machines, prepare leaflets, set up a picket line, and hold the chair in turbulent meetings and were familiar with all the other mechanics indispensable when workers

[1] In *The Communist*, official party organ, Jack Stachel declared in defense of the T.U.U.L. program: "Our basic trade-union policy remains the same. . . . It has nothing in common with traditional dual unionism! We participate actively in all mass trade unions and seek to revolutionize them. The question at issue is one of emphasis. The objective situation demands that we put much more emphasis on the establishment of new unions. . . ."

133

utterly inexperienced in union routines were crowding into halls, clamoring for guidance, chanting "CIO" like three notes in a new litany.

Lewis was confident, of course, that he could outsmart the Stalinists, make them "behave." He had licked them a dozen years running in his own United Mine Workers when the fuzzy-minded, well-meaning, mystical John Brophy had been the spear-point of their opposition to Lewis's dominion. But this time the Miners' chieftain was mistaken. The Browder Bund outsmarted him while he was either asleep at the switch or merely no match for their intrigue. On the surface, for a while, it seemed as if the Stalinists were going to play ball all right. They were willing to fight and to work; and many of them fought hard and worked well and earnestly—but for ulterior purposes. It was soon evident that the well-being and future of American unionism was, and remains in Stalinist circles, secondary to the well-being of the Soviet Union. It was not John L. Lewis and the CIO that claimed their first loyalty. It was Joseph V. Stalin and the U.S.S.R. and the "party line" as it was devised, revised, mortised, and mortified by the Comintern to advance Russia's propaganda and other aims in the United States. Hence the resolutions in union meetings about support for the Spanish Loyalists; hence the efforts to get American workers to boycott Japan; hence the sale of *Fight*, organ of the League Against War and Fascism, Com-

134

munist "front" or "transmission-belt" organization in union halls; hence the injection of issues of "collective security" at meetings where workers were far more anxious to learn something about collective bargaining.

And when in mid 1937 the period of consolidation and stock-taking which followed the CIO's first great organizing drives came round, the Stalinists had obtained positions of trust and authority in the United Automobile Workers, the Transport Workers, the American Communications Association, the Newspaper Guild, the Federation of Architects, Engineers and Technicians, the State, County and Municipal Workers, the National Maritime Union, the Office and Professional Workers, the Woodworkers of America, the Cannery, Agricultural, Packing and Allied Workers, and enough other places to give the Communist Party complete or partial control of at least forty per cent of the CIO's unions. Nor was this Stalinist influence limited to union officials. It extended to Lewis's own kitchen-cabinet advisers such as the ardent party-line sympathizers and fellow travelers Lee Pressman, CIO general counsel, and Len DeCaux, editor of the *CIO News*, official organ, which he transformed into a claque in print for such Stalinists as Joseph Curran of the Maritime Union, Donald Henderson of the Cannery, Agricultural and Packing Workers, Abram Flaxer of the State, County and Municipal Workers, and others who would sell Lewis and American labor down the river at a nod from Holy Joe.

The extent of Stalinist penetration was for some time obscure because party members and their agents within the CIO play safe and dirty. With a fine scorn for any Marquis of Queensberry rules, they hit in the clinches and below the belt. In the belief that their cause is so noble that it warrants any duplicity or treachery, that since a lie is good, the greater the lie the higher the good, they repudiate any affliction, secret or overt, with the Communist Party at the very moment they recite its catechism and count its beads. They call themselves "liberals" or "progressives" or even New Dealers at the very time they are serving the interests of a totalitarian regime. They have developed character-assassination to a bastard art; anyone who exposes or opposes their plots or counter-plots is branded as a janissary of reaction, addicted to the seven deadly sins; until the Hitler-Stalin pact, any such person was a Nazi agent or a Japanese spy.

In the United Automobile Workers, for example, most promising of the CIO's new unions, the Stalinists were anxious and determined to gain ascendancy. They set about wooing the hapless Homer Martin, first preacher head of the union. They told him that if he would only consent to follow the advice and lead of G. K. Gebert, big Stalinist boss in the back room, they would "build him up" into a figure second only to John L. Lewis himself in prominence and prestige. During these "negotiations" the party press and its labor journalists like Bruce Minton and John Stuart were hailing Martin as "vigorous" and "able" and "crisp-spoken" and a "militant" leader of labor. When Martin refused to heed the Stalinist direction, especially in naming their candidates as central-office staff, and when with excellent intentions but meagre mental and "p'litical" equipment he set out to extirpate their influence, they called nearly 160 "wild-cat" strikes simply to embarrass his administration, to paint him as irresponsible, as a weakling. They broke up meetings of the union, fomenting so much discord that it lost more than a third of its original strength. Twice it took all the diplomacy and skilled suasion of Philip Murray and Sidney Hillman to restore some semblance of order out of all this Stalinist-inspired chaos. Meantime, not only in the United Auto Workers union but at least in fifteen more, such typically Stalinist tactics, plus emphasis upon foreign rather than American affairs, disgusted perhaps 400,000 old CIO members, and repelled countless new potential members to such an extent that the CIO began to slide downhill. The loss of membership induced by Stalinist attempts to capture the entire CIO coincided with the post-1937 recession. And this was felt first and most keenly in the very mass-production industries where the CIO had the majority of its adherents, where by the thousand they were laid off, forced on relief, unable to buy enough decent food, let alone pay union dues,

137

a fact which, when linked with Stalinist disruption and the newness and inexperience of many CIO unions, resulted in an overwhelming diminution of income. At the same time the presence of Stalinists in the CIO enabled anti-unionists of all shades, on the basis of "Where's there's smoke, there's fire," to exploit the chance to affix the Red, alien, subversive label to the entire Congress, as they try to affix the same label to any effective agency for collective bargaining. A pamphlet entitled *Join the CIO and Build a Soviet America*, a blatant forgery, was widely circulated by many business groups, including the publicity bureau of the National Association of Manufacturers. Then, too, the Stalinist press, the *Daily Worker*, the *New Masses, The Communist* (monthly journal), kept referring to CIO achievements in a manner that conveyed the impression that the whole show was a Comintern appendage, when actually Stalinists had then no leading positions. Such AFL spokesmen as John P. Frey and Arthur O. Wharton of the Machinists seized upon this data to substantiate their charges that the CIO, from top to bottom, was merely another word for Communism.

First of the CIO high command to appreciate the external and internal havoc wrought by the Stalinists was Sidney Hillman, who had had some bitter experiences with them back in the 1920's when William Z. Foster and his Trade Union Unity League tried to take over New York City's needle trades. He was familiar with their dissemblings, their complete disregard of what happened to a union, the workers, the employers, so long as the party line of the moment was being carried out. Late in 1937 Hillman began a quiet purge of the Stalinists who had slipped under his guard into various posts within the Textile Workers' Organizing Committee, of which he was then chairman. Promptly Philip Murray, head of the Steel Workers' Organizing Committee, followed suit. The United Mine Workers in their 1938 convention passed a resolution barring Stalinists (along with Ku Klux Klan followers) from membership.

The period between the fall of 1937 and the present rise in employment was a time of retrenchment for the CIO, of pulling in sails until the economic storm subsided. Its ruling triumvirate, determined to keep their organization intact, were afraid to risk a fight to the finish against the Stalinists lest in the effort to oust them some forty per cent of the CIO unions be plunged into the kind of strife that is often a preface to disintegration. Nevertheless, rank-and-file rebellions—in the Office Workers, for instance, and in the State, County and Municipal Workers and other places—against Stalinist rule kept breaking out and were smothered by means of "packed" meetings to which whole sections of the Communist Party were invited and where party, not union, causes were advanced and approved. The

139

revolt against the dictatorship which the Stalinists imposed upon every union they controlled widened out and kept growing through 1938 and the next year until on August 23, 1939 it gained a new impetus from an event that at first seemed as if it would shatter the last vestiges of Stalinist hegemony within the CIO.

That event, of course, was the Nazi-Communist nonaggression pact, which resulted in numerous defections among actual party members, such as Granville Hicks, literary critic and Harvard University professor, and among such fellow travelers as Kyle Crichton, *Collier's* movie editor, who in his other manifestation was Robert Forsythe, *New Masses* humorist and author of *Redder than the Rose.* The American Labor Party, overjoyed at the opportunity presented by the Russo-Reich nuptials, moved to jettison its Stalinist cargo and precipitated a knock-down and drag-out fight between Stalinist and anti-Stalinist elements. Other less publicized renunciations and ousters have further depleted Stalinist ranks. Within the CIO, however, the Hitler-Stalin agreement resulted in virtually no public recanting among those who in the past have been identified with the Communist Party line. The widely anticipated upheavals within CIO unions under Stalinist domination never materialized, despite the fact that the new party line calls for a complete *volte-face*, a crusade against "French and British imperialism" and "warmongers like Roosevelt," instead of the former credo of

140

collective security and co-operation with the democracies, among which the Soviet Union was weirdly included.

Yet the CIO 1939 convention sidestepped any public action on this whole issue, while Stalinist "sympathizers" were prominent in the proceedings. But at a secret session of the Executive Board Lewis, prodded by Hillman and Murray, warned against any "dual allegiance" and threatened personally to "put his oar in" any union where the welfare of the workers was subordinated to Communist Party objectives. And to make this warning concrete for those who, in Lewis's own phrase, "think they can make a life work of taking over the CIO for the Communist Party," John Brophy, director of organization for the CIO, and Stalinist cat's-paw, was demoted to the unimportant post of co-ordinating local industrial unions in secondary areas. By the same token Harry Bridges, who had been prominently linked with Stalinist operations, was with a few face-saving remarks booted downstairs, deprived of his job as CIO west-coast director, and confined to California.

Despite this apparent chastisement of the Stalinists, however, they and Lewis would be seeming to play a game of hide-and-seek with each other. The CIO leader proceeds on the assumption that he is "using" them for his own designs; and they are equally confident that they are "using" him and hold him captive. In the first place Lewis feels that he needs their support to carry out his "fight to a finish" against the AFL. The Stalinists are delighted to be of aid and comfort in this "No peace at any price" program; for they are in a panic lest in any reunited labor body their current influence, which is tremendous, could be curtailed to next to nothing. In the second place, Lewis is seeking to launch a national third-party movement that will direct its appeal to the aged, the youth, the unemployed and under-privileged groups, in addition to organized labor itself. His ambitions in this respect play directly into Stalinist hopes that any such political alignment may defeat Roosevelt or the successor he will do much to name in 1940, by draining off enough votes in key states to throw the election to the Republicans. It is ironic, of course, that today the two most vigorously anti-New-Deal factions in the United States are the big-business contributors to the G.O.P. campaign chests on the one hand, and the Stalinists on the other.

The New Deal administration's pro-Allied policy in foreign affairs represents a point of view that the Stalinists within and without the CIO are pledged to hamper and scuttle by every means they can summon. Whatever their protestations to the contrary, they are under the sway of the Soviet Union, and her stake in world politics has first claim upon their energies. They believe that a Republican administration would be more isolationist, less friendly to the Allied cause, and therefore less of an actual or potential threat to the success of the Nazi-Communist alliance, economic, military, political.

To focus our lens clearly on this point, it must be stated unequivocally that Lewis is himself no Communist and has no love for that philosophy. His toleration of their presence in the CIO is personal, not ideational. His aspirations and their instructions happen to dovetail at the moment. He wants to restore a waning political power, to become the spokesman for American isolationists of the "Let's solve our own problems first" school. The Stalinists want a stalemate in the present war; and they are therefore stressing a "Let's stay out of it, let's set our own house in order first" attitude, not to benefit anyone or anything American, but merely to deter and undermine American aid to the Allies, which is a different kettle of fish, and has resulted in vast confusion among the ranks of non-interventionists whose motives are not ulterior.

The CIO is just now recovering in part from its setbacks of 1937, and Lewis is reluctant to subject its internal structure, which requires shoring-up in many places, to any further strains. Still on the defensive, despite his big talk of ten million members in 1944, and with a treasury less than overflowing, he cannot afford to split various CIO segments wide open by a "come hell or high water" anti-Stalinist campaign, especially since he is under the impression that he is finding the

Stalinists useful, at least for the time being.

In any event, to have removed them peremptorily at the 1939 convention, even if he could have done it by means of steam-roller tactics, would not only have turned the assemblage into a witch-hunting bedlam but have offended many CIO anti-Stalinist groups by crushing the democratic principle of "Vote them out" rather than "Throw them out." The advocates of the democratic process in the CIO, and there are many of them, faced still another dilemma: namely, should a man who in his job as labor leader is a first-rate unionist be dumped because of his political belief? Until it can be proved that he has placed political, Stalinist, Lovestonite, Socialist, or other interests above the welfare of his union, shouldn't he be retained and remain entitled to the exercise of free speech and free opinion, however detestable the majority of Americans may think his views to be? Latterly, of course, the anti-Stalinist groups within the CIO, the people who are trying to keep it a democratic organization in accord with American traditions of free speech and fair play, are inclining to the attitude that to raise this kind of question in regard to the Stalinists is merely to beg it; that the Stalinists merely invoke civil liberties as a Trojan Horse and would destroy them as soon as they impeded Stalinist dissemination of a totalitarian doctrine.

Yet the CIO is not alone in its Communist problems,

144

although they are concededly more difficult there than in the AFL. Several of the Federation's own affiliates, however, like the Hotel and Restaurant Workers and various locals of the Painters in the New York City region, have been heavily invaded by Stalinist influences. The AFL, moreover, accepted the dues and the activity of five other Stalinist-controlled unions, such as the Furriers, before they left the Federation for the CIO, of their own free will, not because the AFL spurned their money or their members.

The genuine point at issue, of course, is that a fusion of forces between the AFL and the CIO would give them both, in the very process of merging, an excellent opportunity to weed out their Stalinists and to destroy their power, and thus render a great and invaluable service not alone to the labor movement but to the whole cause of intellectual honesty and moral integrity besides.

CHAPTER VI

THE AFL, THE CIO, AND THE NLRB

PERHAPS NOWHERE else has the struggle between the AFL and the CIO reached such heights of madness, and possibly mutual destruction, as in their behavior toward the National Labor Relations Board. And to place the implications of this lunacy in its proper psycho-pathological context, it is pertinent to review first some of the more general background of the NLRB itself.

The NLRB is, of course, the most vigorously denounced and defended government agency in the United States. On the one hand, its opponents among employers and their great unions, such as the National Association of Manufacturers and the United States Chamber of Commerce, contend that the Board is unfair; that it is one-sided, that it gives labor all the rights

146

and all the breaks, and capital none; that in procedure it is at once judge, jury, and court crier; that it is a preface to the kind of government intervention that must soon or late turn industrial relations in this country into American imitations of the Fascist Syndicates, the Nazi Labor Fronts, the Communist Soviets. Economists of standing in certain limited quarters and Congressmen of unquestioned sincerity have complained that the Board fails, in the very nature of its task, to function on any *pro bono publico* basis and is rather a source of strife, curbing business recovery and frightening away new investments.

On the other hand, the Board's partisans affirm that the very fact that it has been assailed by "interested parties" in different quarters would seem to show that it has been performing its duty in the public interest; that instead of fostering industrial discord, it promotes peace and prosperity; that instead of being in any way a kangaroo court, or dictatorial, it is in its day-to-day behavior the quintessence of the democratic process; that it has endowed millions of Americans with a new sense of dignity and self-respect, of freedom and security in relation to their means of livelihood. The Board's friends deny that, making allowances for the subjective quality of the human mind, it has been influenced by the AFL or CIO in any given case, or by anyone or anything except the desire to apply the law, again granting the limitations of human judgment; or

147

by any motivation except to get at the facts of a particular situation as they are disentangled from passions and prejudices after investigations and hearings at which both management and unions (AFL, CIO, or "non-affiliated") are invited to speak their minds.

Surely, in order to arrive at any fairly impartial estimate of whatever virtues and defects the Board may possess, it is first necessary to try to remove ourselves from this atmosphere of claims and counter-claims, of AFL insistence that the Board is but a CIO auxiliary, of the CIO's conviction that it is becoming an extension of the AFL, of employer hysterics and politician's hanky-panky—an atmosphere as surcharged with emotionalism as a hot showery summer day with heat lightning.

And perhaps in this respect it might help to adopt the method of the literary critic who, when he seeks to assess the merits and shortcomings of a novel, asks himself two vital questions: (1) what has the author set out to do, and (2) how well or how poorly has he done it in terms of content and style? And by this means we can perhaps fashion some reasonably accurate callipers for measuring the Board's worth, or lack of it, for recommending that it be scrapped entirely, or changed in some particulars, or kept intact.

The Board exists, of course, to put into practice the principles of the National Labor Relations Act—more popularly known as the Wagner Act—passed by Con-

148

gress on July 5, 1935 and validated by the Supreme Court on April 15, 1937.

The Act itself was framed to achieve a single underlying purpose: to assure to American workers the right to organize into unions of their own choosing without interference from any source. This, in essence, is all there is to the Wagner Act. It is as simple as that. It is perhaps in its 4,600 words of text the least elaborate measure in the history of American labor legislation— in intent, if not in application.

Its simplicity, however, is on the grand scale, of a kind that has many complex results. The Act has uncovered a Pandora's box of a still controversial issue: namely, is collective bargaining between "capital" and "labor" a good thing or a bad thing for the American people? Does it promote or detract from the national well-being, social, political, economic?

And to lay the groundwork for an answer, let us first define what collective bargaining signifies today. In colloquial terms it means group action by workers who have joined together of their own free will into a union in order to arrange with management the amount of pay they are going to get, and for how many hours of work, and under what conditions. Unionism, of course, is inseparable from collective bargaining; they are Siamese twins.

The process of collective bargaining itself may as-

149

sume many different forms. A single employer may bargain with a number of his workers, as in the case of a restaurant proprietor and his waiters. Or again a group of employers such as building contractors may bargain with a group of unions such as the Carpenters, Painters, Bricklayers, and the like. Or once more an all-inclusive industry-wide association of employers, like that of the coal-mine owners in the Central Competitive Field, may bargain with all their workers through the medium of the all-inclusive United Mine Workers.

Still other variations on this theme are as numerous and diverse as there are kinds of business; the more especially since in this regard unionism is itself a business institution. It is engaged in the co-operative marketing of labor skills, or man-hours. And in its selling operations, its efforts to exact a "reasonable price" for labor energy from the purchaser (the employer), it seeks to substitute group strength for individual weakness. Proponents of the National Labor Relations Act not only accept this thesis in its entirety, but also frequently support it by historical comparisons.

In the early simpler days of American industry, they say in effect, the small workshop was owned and managed by the individual employer or master workman who labored alongside his help. When the question of wage-rates came up it was settled by "higgling," by direct man-to-man exchange of views and offers in a

150

period when there was virtually no difference in knowledge or economic status between employer and employee. Both were familiar with the cost of raw materials, the amount of time and skill required, say, to turn out a pair of shoes or boots. Indeed, in the shoemaking establishment, as in most other manufacture during the early years of the Republic, the worker owned his own means of employment, the tools of his trade, his knife and awl and pincers, his hammer and lapstone and stirrup and all the rest. Moreover, in a growing country, with free lands readily available, with the whole economy expanding at a rapid pace, he had a choice of alternatives if he wasn't satisfied with his job. In the first place, he could easily get another; for during the first few decades of our national life the demand for labor in one locality more than offset any surplus in another, by and large. In the second place, the worker could set up shop for himself to serve the needs of a multiplying population in new and old communities, going into business with a hundred dollars, more or less, saved from earnings. In the third place, he could move westward toward the always receding frontier, and like thousands of other pioneers he could "chop, root, and plant" the acres for his own clearing and become a farmer, or perhaps go prospecting for gold.

In any case, since he was able to turn to a new boss, or to a number of new pursuits, he was reasonably sure that he could always earn a living, often a quite comfortable living, in fact. And with some few exceptions, notably in textiles, his bargaining power was equal to that of his employer and it was easy enough to reach an agreement satisfactory to both sides.

Today, however, all this has been drastically, if not completely, changed. It has been changing with an ever increasing momentum since before the Civil War. In modern large-scale industry, for example, the individual bargain, premised upon two equally strong and independent "contracting parties," has become virtually extinct. From the 1870's forward, in particular, the stock-company and corporation supplanted the individually owned and managed store, mine, mill, factory, shipyard, and latterly even farms, moving inexorably toward that integration of control symbolized in 1901 with the formation of United States Steel, our first billion-dollar company. Side by side with this trend toward consolidation marched the use of new labor-saving machinery which cost relatively vast sums to install. And the need for such outlays itself contributed to more and yet more mergers and combinations, calling for still further aggregations of capital. All this, of course, has been a process of natural growth in the evolution of American industry from a semi-handicraft to a "factoryized" and to its present mass-production stage. During the last phase of this transformation, the worker has been divorced from the ownership of tools, his means of self-employment, and from the opportunities inherent in the free lands, while all they signified are gone.

In a modern shoe plant, for example, he works with equipment that may cost $100,000 a year merely to rent, and where in the bottoming department alone, which is one of the six basic divisions in today's shoe manufacture, there are buffers, edge-setters, heel-burnishers, scourers, McKay sewers, and many more. They are classed as unskilled, or at best semi-skilled. They own only their ability to work; and with the mounting mechanization of industry, individual capacities and differences in diligence and initiative are reduced to a dead level of sameness. All the copy-book maxims of application, alertness, sticking at it, are useless as a ladder to advancement; for when the finished product is ready for packing, who can tell whether John Jones or Bill Smith is the superior worker? When a completed car rolls off the assembly line, what criteria exist to single individual merit out of the result of multiple enterprise? And it would seem at least significant that in great mass-production industries no executive of standing above straw-boss or foreman has come up from conveyor-belt ranks; the Knudsens belonged to a category of specialized mechanics whose function is dwindling; other corporation executives are former salesmen, or engineers, or technicians, or publicity experts, not men who have come up from the "line." Am-

153

bition, hard work, sobriety, steadiness, and all the related virtues suffice only for the negative purpose of holding on to a semi-automatic job, not the affirmative purpose of getting up in the world. Under the impact of the new technology, especially since the end of the first World War, the American worker has been forced into living on a static plane of "status" rather than upon his forebear's more flexible plane of choices implicit in relatively greater opportunity. Separately or together, workers lack the funds for acquiring the costly machinery of today's far-flung corporate undertakings. No single worker can, like his spiritual ancestor, threaten to employ himself. If dissatisfied with his lot, his chance to turn to alternatives is rigorously limited, and is almost non-existent in times of depression.

Under such conditions there is no such thing as bargaining for the solitary unorganized worker, with a few negligible exceptions. The management of a particular plant, after weighing the factors which enter into its costs of production, and the dividends it must pay, decides upon a certain wage-scale. For the average job-seeker who applies at the hiring office on Monday morning it is "take it or leave it." He can rarely do anything else. He is, to be sure, legally free to sell his labor on whatever terms he thinks best. But this liberty is all but meaningless in view of the chronic over-supply of labor, from population increase and immigration, in America during the past forty years, except for the period of the first World War and seven years of its boom aftermath.

The worker and his family are human beings; they need to eat, to be sheltered and clothed; and to satisfy such minimum requirements money is imperative. Unless the worker belongs to the small group of the exceptionally skilled, or those with savings in the bank, he accepts what he is offered because there are plenty of others who will if he won't.[1]

Certainly, the worker in this instance hasn't bargained on any equal footing. Unlike the employer, he hasn't access to data concerning overhead, prices of supplies, interest on investment, obsolescence, and the other elements which go to make up the "prevailing wage." It may be fair, and even generous, as it quite often is; or it may be far less than the job is worth. In any case, lacking this knowledge, and lacking any influence over the use of the producing "tools," and without income-creating property of his own, he is distinctly at a disadvantage.

Gradually workers by trial-and-error methods, seeking to adapt themselves for more secure survival amid the ever changing environment of industry, hit upon what they felt was the only possible alternative to this kind of bargaining. Long ago they discovered that if

[1] It has been estimated that even if 1929 production levels should be maintained throughout 1940, there will be 124 workers available for every 83 jobs, as the result of economies in operation and technological displacement of man-power during the past ten years.

they were to have anything to say about their wages and hours and work-conditions, the individual form of bargaining had to be superseded by the collective bargain. They would, in short, have to stop competing against one another. They would have to call a halt to taking the lowest bid from the lowest bidder. They would have to formulate and pledge themselves to abide by wage-scales and hour-schedules which represented to greater or less extent their desires and their participation. Instead of acting each man for himself, they would have to act in concert, on a basis of mutual aid and protection. Their choice was either to submit to the discipline and authority of their own group—namely the union, in which they had a voice and a vote —or to submit to the authority of "the company," sometimes benevolent and sometimes tyrannical, but always capricious, and in the conduct of which they had no control. In brief, they found out that under individual bargaining the strength of the group was no greater than that of its weakest member.[1]

Moreover, the workers observed, the employer could readily dispense with the services of John Jones, who all by himself objected to existing arrangements; but if

[1] Conversely, this is not true of the weak employer, nor is the employer group threatened by its weakest member, at least over the short-run. Rather, it is considerably helped; for the latter, usually on the ragged edge of bankruptcy, is under terrific pressure to lower costs by cutting wages. He is likely therefore to be especially obdurate in dealing with the wage-earner's demand for a "decent" living.

156

John Jones and ten or a hundred or a thousand or more of his fellows banded together in a union and objected, and threatened to withdraw their labor-power, all together and all at once, the employer could not discharge them with anywhere near the same ease, without risking delay in filling his orders, and the loss of customers and profits.

In any such contest, of course, the employer—whether individual or collective—has a certain "staying-power" implicit in cash reserves, credit facilities, the ability to purchase strikebreakers by the carload. He may decide to "wait it out" by suspending operations entirely. Since the overwhelming majority of workers are but a few days removed from want, he may feel that hunger may "bring them to their senses" and soon force them back to their jobs. This "Starve-'em-out" tactic was enormously successful prior to the establishment of Federal Home Relief, and is the chief reason why various employer interests oppose this aid by such rationalizations as that it "undermines morale" by keeping "loafers" idle; for if a striker's family does not suffer too unendurable pangs of hunger, he is less tractable, more willing to stand up for what he believes are his rights. However, in spontaneous strikes, when the employees are unorganized and are not guided by professionals, the employer is often able to bring enough pressure upon local politicians to prevent any relief to his strikers. On the other hand, when a union calls a

157

strike, it is by its very nature prepared to check this "Starve 'em out" strategy on the employer's part. Its officials would raise holy hell by various publicity means if relief is denied through the employer's intercession. Moreover, by means of its dues, the union has accumulated a treasury of strike reserves which can as a rule keep its adherents in bread at least while differences are being ironed out. It is also able to support full-time leaders who in general devote themselves to looking out for the organization's interests. They study the labor market. They keep informed as to costs and prices. They are experts in bargaining who can meet with employers across the conference table and discuss moot points with knowledge and insight.

In essence it is this mobilizing of labor's economic strength for settling the terms of employment that is collective bargaining. It includes not only the making of agreements which specify the whens and wherefores of the management-union relationship over a given interval, but also their enforcement as well.

The legislators and economists who framed the National Labor Relations Act assumed that under the present-day structure of American industry collective bargaining was not only valuable but also indispensable if a new baron-serf relationship (without the serf's security) were to be avoided by the American worker. They pointed out further that in the highly competitive sectors of industry, such as textiles, collective bargain-

158

ing was needed to help the employer stabilize his business in relation to his rivals, and pay his labor what from the ethical standpoint he would prefer to pay, and to prevent exploitation, the sweat-shop practice of "taking it out of labor's hide." In the more stable, usually better financed, semi-monopolistic industries such as steel, collective bargaining was needed to obtain from great corporate employers what they could well afford to pay. The Act's advocates affirmed that this program not only would protect the worker in the exercise of his rights as a citizen of industry and as a citizen of the United States but also would in the long run lay the foundation for a mutually constructive and satisfactory and smoother-running association between employer and employee.

From such premises, the Act's sponsors declared that collective bargaining should be encouraged by the federal government and incorporated into national policy. They asserted also that industrial peace, the uninterrupted turning of wheels, and the more regular exchange of goods and services that this engenders, were vital to the creation of any sound, lasting prosperity. But the amity between employers and employees was constantly disrupted by strikes, the overwhelming majority of which derived directly or indirectly from the employer's refusal to "recognize" unions, to permit their formation, to bargain collectively.

In thus declining to deal with his workers, said the Act's authors, the employer was taking an undue advantage of his control over job-opportunities. When under such conditions the wage-bargain was struck, the scales were tipped in his favor. He held all the trumps. The wage-earner without benefit of a union to speak up for him was utterly helpless. The two participants in the transaction, the employer and the worker, were unequal in their ability to exert economic pressure.

The National Labor Relations Act was designed to rectify this imbalance, to restore the process of bargaining to the two-sided plane of "equals" contending upon approximately equal terms.

The Act established the National Labor Relations Board as the instrumentality for achieving this objective. The Board, despite attacks upon it as something at once startling and sinister in its novelty, is on the contrary no innovation. Its antecedents go back to the industrial commissions of 1898 and 1908; to the regulation of capital-labor relations in the railroad industry, beginning in 1888; to the War Labor Boards of 1917–'18, to its immediate predecessors, the various Labor Boards developed during the NRA period. It reflects some fifty years of government experience and experiment in promoting more harmonious industrial relations in the United States. It is the arch-type of the recent quasi-judicial administrative agencies which are crucially and increasingly needed as policemen guiding the ever more crowded traffic of our social and economic life.

The Board is composed of three non-labor, non-employer specialists in industrial relations, appointed by the President with the advice and consent of the Senate. The Board has on its roster some 800 central headquarters and field and regional employees, such as attorneys, examiners, investigators, trial attorneys, along with a staff of economists, statisticians, and research workers and a Bureau of Public Information, which is its publicity division. The Board costs the people of the United States about $2,700,000 a year.

The Board's present chairman is Joseph Warren Madden, former Dean of the Law School at West Virginia University. When he was head of the mediation committee which in 1934 successfully resolved the Pittsburgh street-car dispute, Madden imparted to hearings that might otherwise have got out of hand the folksy, gallus-hitching atmosphere of a small-town court where the judge, sprawling over his bench, is settling a fuss and trying to keep everybody friends. Today he retains much of this quality. He is quiet, reflective, and frequently conveys the impression that he is tired, or even abstracted, or a-hankering to go fishin', when in reality he is only a little less attentive

161

and relaxed than a steel trap at the moment of being sprung. He came to the Board with a profound faith in the honesty and good sportsmanship of industry and labor alike, and he has held to this attitude despite discouragement, despite the fact that it was rudely jarred almost immediately after he had assumed his post as Board chairman. For one of the very first Board hearings at which he presided was that of the Fruehauf Trailer Company and the United Automobile Workers Federal Labor Union No. 19375. Testimony in this case, which lasted from November 6 to December 12, 1935, among other things revealed that the management had hired a Pinkerton detective to work in its factory and, in the phrase of the company's vice-president, "to ferret out the union activities of the men" and to keep the company "informed of what was going on." But this operative did even better than that, it appeared. He got himself elected treasurer of the union, furnished the company with the names of active unionists, who were then discharged, used his office to deflect union policies to the company's advantage, and finally embezzled the union's funds—this last something he was not instructed to do.

At this juncture Mr. Madden, who was visibly appalled, amazed Fruehauf attorneys by suggesting that since the company was responsible for hiring the Pinkerton espionage agent, it should at least make good the loss of the money he had stolen from the union.

162

But this display of righteous indignation had curious results. From that day forward, and mainly on the basis of his behavior in the Fruehauf episode, Madden has been assailed as "unfair to business" and biased toward labor, a somewhat saddening commentary on the state of American business morals.

Still shocked by the Fruehauf revelations, Madden some time later made a speech before the Congress of American Industry. "Under these conditions," he then declared, "it is remarkable that among the leaders of newly organized [union] groups there are as few hotheads and zealots as there are. And to the extent that new leadership is unwise, it seems to me that the cure is as obvious as the cause. Let the employer make known by word and conduct to his workers that they have the right to organize and meet without interference, that any employee may act like a man and take a man's part in the determination of his affairs, and sound leadership will inevitably emerge. If this be not a sound prediction, the whole basis of American democracy is false." The applause on this occasion was restrained, but Madden has not swerved from the implications of this point of view.

Nor has Edwin S. Smith, second ranking member of the Board in length of service. He is not a lawyer, but is a hold-over from the National Labor Relations Board of NRA days. Blunt, bright, somewhat bellicose in appearance and manner, he has drawn employer maledictions as a "radical," while the AFL consistently has accused him of sitting up nights to find ways and means of favoring the CIO. He earned his labor stripes as a personnel director in Boston, and as the former Commissioner of Labor and Industries for the state of Massachusetts. He is the Board's most hard-hitting opponent of various amendments to the National Labor Relations Act which aim at separating the Board's judicial from its administrative functions. He affirmed recently that any such proposals "reach far beyond the Wagner Act and strike at the very heart of the administrative process.

"The National Labor Relations Board," he continued, "like other quasi-judicial agencies, is primarily an investigating and fact-finding body with authority to require, but only with court approval, the remedying of wrongs that have been committed. The building up of the Board's administrative procedures is closely linked with its judicial functions. One of the chief virtues of quasi-judicial agencies," he added, "specializing in a particular field, is supposed to be that their judicial decisions are constantly vitalized and brought closer to reality by the intimate acquaintance of their members with the day-to-day realities that administrative supervision brings. I am very much afraid that the separation of administrative and judicial functions would lead not only to an unfortunate disharmony between two branches of government, both working for a common end, but to a large extent would produce a semi-sterilization of the opinion-making branch. I firmly believe," he went on, "that what the National Labor Relations Act and the Board require for the future are not amendments but time for the growing employer acceptance of the Act to crystallize."

The third member of the Board, Dr. William M. Leiscrson, quondam Antioch economist, also defends the Act, but is less enthusiastic over certain phases and personalities in its administration. He is a baldish, gnome-like, pipe-smoking, philosophic man, although the CIO doubts his famed "detachment" and assails him for leaning toward the AFL. He is by temperament a referee; and as the brains of the National Mediation Board, which supervises industrial relations on the country's railroads, he had gained a tremendous reputation for the application of constructive horse sense in management-union affairs. He was somewhat hurriedly transferred from the National Mediation Board to the National Labor Relations Board, less to replace the retiring Donald Wakefield Smith [1] than to become the lightning-rod for the shafts of criticism that began forking over the NLRB's roof in the spring of 1939.

He believes that "much of the conflict over the NLRB" would be clarified if the entire system of gov-

[1] Mr. Smith is today a special counsel for the Ford Motor Company, specializing in its labor cases.

165

ernment mediation were revamped and enlarged, since many disputes brought to the Labor Board more properly belong to a mediation agency rather than one with the right to declare what the law is. He feels that the chief defect of the Board at present is that it is operated on the theory "of the novel where, after the hero and heroine get together, they live happily ever after, whereas anyone who is married knows that's not true." And to supply more realism and guidance to the post-honeymoon period, he would like to see machinery similar to that used for mediation in the railway and maritime boards set up alongside the NLRB, to supplement its activity. He thinks that the Department of Labor's Conciliation Bureau is entirely inadequate to this purpose, not only in the smallness of its staff, but also in its excessively limited powers.

In all of this he is anxious to place the Board's accent more upon mutually satisfactory day-to-day adjustments between industry and labor, rather than upon the narrow legalistic emphasis given this question by Nathan Witt, Board secretary. It has been Witt who, as personnel clearing-house for the Board, did much to staff it with unripe young lawyers who had fine academic backgrounds, but who tended to be arid, bookish, and to take too strictly a juristic rather than a humanistic view of labor relations. They knew too much about Blackstone, too little about people. Altogether too many of the Board's secondary and tertiary representatives had never before met employers or foremen or workers face to face and therefore dealt in abstractions labeled "Capital" and "Labor" rather than with human beings embodying both, and all gradations in between.

Moreover, Witt—known as the "human bottleneck" through whom applicants for minor Board posts had to pass for approval—is said often to have imposed his own peculiar criteria, sympathy for the Communist Party line, as a job-prerequisite. Together with the smart, arrogant Lee Pressman, CIO general counsel, Witt has been repeatedly accused, despite repeated denials, of seeking to transform Board appointments into a patronage mill for the Stalinist faction within the CIO. He has a sly turn of mind, and his urge toward intrigue is seemingly invincible. Equally invincible, and more publicized, is his urge to self-confession. He has often tended to use NLRB stationery as a personal diary; and his guesses, his gossip, are mingled with "routine" communications. During the Smith Committee's investigation of the NLRB, Witt's associates lived in momentary fear that the details of his personal life would be turning up in inter-office memoranda.

Until recently he has been able to hoodwink his superiors on the Board; but with the accession of Leiserson, Witt's indiscretions—political and otherwise —have been rigorously held in check, and his days as Board secretary are numbered. Certainly the blackest mark on the Madden-Smith escutcheon has been their naïve and over-amiable toleration of Witt and his devious modality.

The least known but perhaps the most significant personality in the entire NLRB is David J. Saposs, its chief economist and director of its division of economic research. He is America's leading authority on labor. A quiet, almost shy man, with a mop of whitening hair, he has brought to the NLRB the patient, probing, yet creative intelligence of the great scholar as against the mere scholastic. An active unionist in his youth, he later became research assistant to Professor John R. Commons at Wisconsin University and collaborated in the monumental *History of Labor in the United States.* He is personally the author of *Readings in Trade Unionism,* an indispensable handbook; *Left-Wing Unionism,* an impartial survey of labor's radicals; and *The Labor Movement in Post-War France,* a study prepared for Columbia University's Council for Social Research, and the best available in English. He has spent twenty years traveling in all the forty-eight states, observing labor conditions at first hand for New York State's Department of Labor, for the Interchurch World Movement, for the United States Commission on Industrial Relations, for the Carnegie and Rockefeller Foundations. Yet his unique contribution to the NLRB stems less from his almost ideally balanced training for his post than from his dramatizing of the

168

need to complement legal arguments with economic analysis based upon concrete, integrated, irrefutable facts. By means of a research at once painstaking and profound, he has quickened and enlarged the concept of law as the realistic and immediately responsive reflection of living economic processes, rather than a litany for the long dead; and it may well be that future historians will refer to his pioneering in this direction as the most important single development in today's administrative process as embodied in the NLRB and similar agencies.

A good many corporations might have succeeded in evading application of the Wagner Act to their own labor relations were it not for the Saposs technique of making economic research one of the most useful tools in the whole NLRB kit. The Borden Company, for example, claimed exemption from the Wagner Act on the ground that it did not engage in interstate commerce and therefore could not come under the jurisdiction of a national law which, according to its own preamble, was designed "To diminish the causes of labor disputes burdening or obstructing interstate commerce. . . ." And at first glance it appeared as if the NLRB lacked authority to consider the unfair labor practices with which the Borden Company was charged, since the bulk of the milk it distributed was purchased from New York State farmers and consumed in New York City. Furthermore, a previous court decision (*Nebbia* v. *New York* [291 U.S. 502]) had stressed the localized character of New York's milk supply and the need for state regulation of the industry. Saposs and his staff, however, went to the Federal Trade Commission and the Securities Exchange Commission and turned up a vast quantity of material showing that the Borden Company was but part of a big corporation with many branches throughout the United States. Saposs and his aides prepared an elaborate series of maps, charts, and graphs to indicate the location of these subsidiaries, and Borden's own umbilical attachment to the parent concern. The Saposs findings further showed that Borden's regularly received and sold cheese, butter, eggs, and the like from outside New York State. At the same time, scrutiny of milk-inspection dates as filed with the health departments of Stamford, Connecticut, and Newark, New Jersey, and elsewhere disclosed, according to the final Saposs report, "that a major portion of the [Borden Company] milk originated or passed through New Jersey, Pennsylvania, Vermont, Connecticut or Massachusetts before being delivered in New York City.

"It was further shown," the report continued, "by advertisements of the company and from other sources that Borden's owned and operated more than 60 country milk-receiving stations to which farmers delivered milk" and from which "it was shipped by Borden's in its own tank cars by railroad, or by contract truck carrier.

"It was thus evident," the summary concludes, "that a company which by superficial examination appeared to be engaged only in retail trade not only received products in interstate commerce but was also directly engaged in interstate transportation, and that a strike of its employees would clearly interrupt interstate commerce." The sequel to this investigation was that the Borden Company, when presented with this evidence, agreed to cease and desist from the acts complained of and reinstated sixteen employees with back pay.

The recent attacks upon Saposs and his division by Congressional reactionaries are a belated and backhanded recognition of the crucial nature of the work he has done; and that to hamper it, or to destroy it, is the quickest possible way of smashing the effectiveness of the NLRB. And in their efforts to discredit him the Congressional foes of the NLRB and all it symbolizes have stooped to the duplicity of calling Saposs a Communist when any look at any record would have shown him to be perhaps the most consistent enemy of Communists and fellow travelers in all official Washington. In Communist Party circles for a generation the very mention of his name has been a signal for a hymn of hate. They are the antithesis of everything he repre-

171

sents: the free spirit of human inquiry into the need for social and economic changes which are to be achieved within the framework of the democratic process and under the Constitution of the United States. It is a tragic and minatory thing that the Toland V. Smiths, the Earl Browders, and the Fritz Kuhns should all join hands in seeking to traduce the ablest technician in the field of labor relations that this country has so far produced.

II

Contrary to a widespread impression, the Board does not mediate, or adjust grievances, as did the NRA boards, except informally. It does not arbitrate, or compel both sides to reach an agreement over a controversial point. It has nothing directly to do with accident-prevention, or workmen's compensation, or with other pigments entering into the capital-labor picture. All these are left to the appropriate state and federal agencies.

Nor does the Board prevent employers from proceeding against unions in the courts by means of civil suits for damages or from getting out injunctions to restrain union activity of one kind or another. Actually, under the provisions of the National Labor Relations Act, the Board has been assigned two major functions. In the first place, it is to prohibit employers from resorting to five "unfair labor practices" enumerated in the

172

Act as thwarting the right to bargain collectively. In brief, the Board must see to it that an employer doesn't impede, coerce, or otherwise interfere with his workers in their efforts to form a union of their own choosing. He cannot finance or otherwise dominate any labor organization within his purview. He cannot use his hire-and-fire ability either to encourage or to discourage membership in a union. He cannot demote, discharge, or otherwise discriminate against an employee who has testified against him or filed a complaint against him at a Board hearing. He must bargain in good faith with the spokesmen duly selected by his workers, but—and this a point often overlooked—he is not required to reach an agreement. In short, no matter how philanthropic an employer's motivation may be, he must—toward the question of unionism on his premises—"keep his hands off."

In the second place, under Section 9 of the Act, the Board has the duty of ascertaining the "unit appropriate for collective bargaining," whether it should be the "employer unit," or all workers within a given enterprise, or a "craft unit" of workers of certain distinctive occupation, or a "plant unit" or all workers at a particular mill or mine, or whatever. Once this proper unit has been decided on, it is "certified" (by methods to be indicated later) as the exclusive bargaining agent for the majority of employees at a given establishment, leaving room, however, for any minority group who may want their grievances remedied by other means, such as their own personal consultation with the employer.

In the exercise of both these basic functions the Board has had to face some extremely vexing problems. It has had to interpret the Act in accord with its intent, since the blanket "simplicity" of its coverage, its broad catch-all character, rendered it difficult to codify any rigid rules in advance, the chief reason, of course, why the Act is almost impossible to evade. The Board therefore has had to invoke its own discretion over a wide range of issues, in part because industrial relations consist of intensely "human" adjustments, and in part because the Board had few precise precedents; it has had to "create the living law" by seeking to apply a general principle to a specific situation, a fact that has aroused some highly hysterical criticism of its procedure. That procedure, as it relates to the unfair practices of Section 8, for example, conforms in general to the following pattern.

An employee, but more often a labor organization, goes to one of the Board's twenty-two regional offices, located from Maine to Hawaii, and files a charge of unfair labor practices against an employer.[1] A Board field examiner investigates the situation, talking with both the employer and the workers involved. About half of all Board cases are dismissed at this juncture,

[1] The Board itself is not empowered to initiate cases.

174

either because evidence is lacking to support the allegation, or because the employer and his workers decide to get together and bury the hatchet by themselves.

If this happier result is not forthcoming, the Board's investigator and regional head communicate with the employer. They tell him that there is a substantial amount of evidence to sustain his workers' contention. Then the Board members try to persuade him to reconsider before they issue a formal complaint against him. Although—as previously indicated—mediation is not officially a duty of the Board, its agents are often successful in disposing of cases by soothing down ruffled wattles and by placing unguents on injured egos on both sides of the fence, and in general by trying to inject a note of calm and goodwill. The Postal Telegraph Company and the International Shoe Company cases are merely better known among the thousands settled thus informally at this point in the Board's procedure.

If, however, this oral, extra-curricular suasion fails to change the employer's mind, the regional director issues a complaint against him, citing in detail the unfair labor practices attributed to him. He is then given a number of weeks in which to prepare his answer, which, item by item, is to be delivered at a hearing before a trial examiner who is appointed by the central office in Washington. In other words, a brand-new Board official prosecutes the case in order to avoid unconscious collusion, and to create a *cordon sanitaire,* between the Board's fact-finders and its pleaders in any situation.

At this hearing—only five and a half per cent of all Board cases ever get this far, the rest dropping out by the wayside en route—the employer may summon his own witnesses. He (usually his counsel) may cross-examine the Board's witnesses. Any unions concerned in the dispute may also participate. A few cases, notably that of the Borden Company, are settled amicably at this stage of the game. If not, the trial examiner turns out what is called an "intermediate" report, a summation of arguments pro and con, and everybody involved is granted time to pick it to pieces. Then this report, by now as bulky as a *Britannica,* by virtue of comment, addenda, footnotes by all sides, is shipped to Washington, where it is gone over with a fine-tooth comb by the Board's special-review section. Finally, the whole affair is reviewed personally by the three top-ranking members of the Board itself.

At this point, too, a number of firms, among them the United Fruit Company, the Solvay Process Company, and the General Chemical Company, have been absolved of charges brought against them. As a rule, however, relatively few cases are dismissed in full when they reach the heights of hearing before this triune tribunal.

If the Board finds the employer guilty as charged,

he is once more urged to bring himself within the law, to avoid further litigation. But if he then refuses to comply with the Board's interpretation of the law, upon the evidence submitted, the Board releases a "cease and desist" order and petitions a circuit court of appeals to enforce it by an order of its own. This court has virtually unlimited power, in the light of arguments presented by the employer and the Board, to modify, to set aside, or affirm the Board's decision. In short, the Board cannot enforce its orders without recourse to the courts—a tradition long established by the administrative agencies of the federal government, from the Interstate Commerce Commission, to the Federal Trade Commission, to the NLRB itself. And if the employer feels himself aggrieved, he too may look to the courts for relief and may carry the issues of his own case up to the very Supreme Court. It is only after a circuit court of appeals has upheld the Board's findings—action which may take anywhere from two months to two years after the filing of the original charge—that the employer is under effective compulsion to obey the law.

In general, cases which come before the Board fall into three broad categories. The first involves the "complaint" or unfair labor practice cases. The second covers the increasingly vital "representation" cases which have to do with the "appropriate unit" for collective bargaining and in which the Board has been caught in the crossfire of AFL-CIO strife, a contingency hardly anticipated when the Act was drawn. In the third group are the much publicized, much misunderstood "contract" cases which combine features of both the "complaint" and "representation" types and concern collusion and fraud between an employer and a union in signing a collective-bargaining pact.

In considering each in turn, it must be kept in mind that the Board can restrict the employer's conduct in only one particular: anti-union activity. Otherwise he can hire and fire workers as he sees fit. He can select or reject them on the basis of their competence, their age, their religion, their race, the cut of their clothes, or because he likes or dislikes their political opinions. He can close down, dismantle, reorganize, refurbish, enlarge, contract, or relocate his plant for any reason except anti-union activity.

The Board therefore has to distinguish between antiunion behavior and the normal legitimate actions of an employer in running his business. And as a microcosm to illustrate this problem consider the following case:

In New York City the proprietor of the Omaha Hat Corporation, named Novgorod, discharged two of his workers, Magzamen and Rivoli, hat-finishers, on July 13, 1937. He claimed that the two men were incompetent. They were slow, he said, and careless, quite the worst in the shop. On the other hand, they asserted that they were fully capable and that they had been discharged for their efforts in trying to build a local of the United Hat Workers Union (AFL) in their plant. On their behalf the union filed a complaint at the Board's regional office in downtown Manhattan.

Upon inquiry the Board discovered that the owner had been conducting a successful anti-unionization campaign among his employees for five years. To discredit the idea of unionism itself, he had personally, with the aid of two *agents provocateurs*, precipitated two strikes which he had quickly broken by means of injunctions, as a warning against the perils of united action on the part of the workers. And this for a time quelled the union zeal of his labor force. But when an upsurge of union sentiment was reported to him by his own stool-pigeons, he tried to fashion a "safety-valve" with which to head it off. He set up the Omahaian Social Club, a company union, with the avowed object of "fostering a spirit of fraternity among the men." But he himself paid the membership dues and other incidental expenses. Together with his attorney he drew up an agreement between himself and his workers, stipulating various wage-rates and shop rules. Shortly thereafter he himself reneged this pact, and reduced wages, and at the same time dissolved the club.

Whereas he insisted that he had been compelled to discharge Magzamen and Rivoli for ineptness, the

179

Board's survey of the situation showed something else again. It found that the pay of both men compared favorably with that of other hat-finishers in the plant —an important point, since both were paid on piece rates. Their relatively high, above-average earnings therefore proved that, far from being maladroit, they were very expert indeed. Testimony offered by the foreman and other workers disclosed that hat-finishers who were unable to maintain a certain standard in speed and quality were dismissed within a few days. But both Magzamen and Rivoli had held their jobs for a year or longer. In addition, the former, some weeks prior to his dismissal on the ground of inefficiency, had been told by his superior that the "boys had better stop talking." And two days before discharging Rivoli he asked him from whom he had obtained the application blank for joining the union.

"Why do you want to know these men?" Rivoli inquired.

"Well, Joe," retorted the foreman, "I like to know. . . . These men have to get fired."

"Listen," said Rivoli, "I quit job but you never know from my mouth who told me join union." Both Magzamen and Rivoli further stated that they had been positively "squealed on" by the employer's spies, since membership in the union was kept secret for fear of the retaliation of the pink slip.

And while this whole film was being reeled off on

the Board's screen, and the union was making head-way in organizing hitherto frightened employees, the owner closed down his New York plant and prepared to transfer operations to Garwood, New Jersey. Upon sifting the facts from this setting, the Board ordered both Magzamen and Rivoli reinstated with back pay from the date of their discharge. During the past four and a half years the Board has encountered thousands of cases similar in spirit, though different in scope, but with the essentials almost always the same. In every instance the discharge of actual or potential unionists has been accompanied by collateral evidence defi-nitely demonstrating the employer's anti-union bias.

In general in applying Section 8,[1] the Board has held that the employer, to frustrate collective bargaining, may not use labor spies to worm themselves into unions and report on their plans and policies, a practice financed by American industry to the tune of thirty million dollars a year until the exposures of the La

[1] Section 8 of the National Labor Relations Act states that "It shall be an unfair labor practice for an employer (1) to interfere with, restrain, or coerce employees [in the exercise of the rights guaranteed in Section 7]. . . . (2) To dominate or interfere with the formation or administration of any labor organization or con-tribute financial or other support to it. . . . (3) By discrimination in regard to hire or tenure of employment or any term or condition of employment to encourage or discourage membership in any labor organization. . . . (4) To discharge or otherwise discriminate against an employee because he has filed charges or given testimony under this Act. . . . (5) To refuse to bargain collectively with the repre-sentatives of his employees.

181

Follette Committee, investigating civil liberties, provoked such public revulsion that much of this espionage activity has been presumably curtailed, when not abolished. The employer cannot instruct his agents, private detectives, or criminals, or "nobles" or "finks," to foster strike violence to blow up railroad tracks or smash windows and then blame union "agitators" for it all, one of the favorite devices of altogether too many American employers. He cannot circulate blacklists containing the names of workers discharged for union sympathies and described as "trouble-makers," thus depriving them of their means of getting a new job. He cannot hire gorillas to shoot, stab, club to death, or otherwise murder unionists or to do them physical injury. He cannot propagandize his employees against unionism by calling organizers "a bunch of Reds who want to overthrow the government" or "racketeers who wear diamonds big as marbles and live off workers' dues," or either or both.

And it is, of course, this restraint placed by the Board upon vilifying unions, or upon threatening workers with reprisals should they join one, that has evoked a tremendous to-do about the exercise of "free speech." Yet it is difficult to see how this form of anti-union activity differs essentially from other influences coming under the head of "coercion" and "interference." Nor can the employer discriminate against unionists by evicting them from company-owned houses, or persuading grocers to cut off credit when unionists are striking. Despite all this, however, employers still are getting rid of workers who favor unionism. Often a new medical examination of a plant's employees reveals, against the law of averages, that unionists are without exception physically unfit and thus must be laid off. Or customers of a particular plant will suddenly start writing letters that they will give no more orders if the enterprise "goes union," communications which are discreetly shown around, although the employer previously may have revealed little or no inclination to let his workers see his correspondence.

And naturally the persistence of this behavior raises the question why the American employer—whether an actual flesh-and-blood person or the fictional person of a corporation—has resisted unionism with such violence and irresponsibility in the past, and even continues the process in the present against the explicit fiat of a national law approved by Congress and by the Supreme Court.

Specifically it raises the question why the president of Remington Rand, Inc., would first devise and later distribute to the members of the National Association of Manufacturers his own streamlined "Mohawk Valley Formula" for fending off unionism—a "formula" summarized by the NLRB as follows:

First: When a strike is threatened, label the union leaders as "agitators" to discredit them with the public and their

183

own followers. In the plant, conduct a forced balloting under the direction of a foreman in an attempt to ascertain the strength of the union and to make possible misrepresentation of the strikers as a small minority imposing their will on the majority. At the same time, disseminate propaganda, by means of press releases, advertisements, and the "activities of 'missionaries,'" such propaganda falsely stating the issues involved in the strike so that the strikers appear to be making arbitrary demands, and the real issues, such as the employers' refusal to bargain collectively, are obscured. Concurrently with these moves, by exerting economic pressure through threats to move the plant, align the influential members of the community into a cohesive group opposed to the strike. Include in this group, usually designated a "Citizens' Committee," representatives of the bankers, real estate owners and business men, i.e., those most sensitive to any threat of removal of the plant because of its effect on property values and purchasing power flowing from pay rolls.

Second: When the strike is called, raise high the banner of "law and order," thereby causing the community to mass legal and police weapons against a wholly imagined violence and to forget that those of its members who are employees have rights equal with the other members of the community.

Third: Call a "mass meeting" of the citizens to coordinate public sentiment against the strike and to strengthen the power of the Citizens' Committee, which organization, thus supported, will both aid the employer in exerting pressure upon the local authorities and itself sponsor vigilante activities.

Fourth: Bring about the formation of a large armed

184

police force to intimidate the strikers and to exert a psychological effect on the citizens. This force is built up by utilizing local police, State Police if the Governor cooperates, vigilantes and special deputies, the deputies being chosen if possible from other neighborhoods so that there will be no personal relationships to induce sympathy for the strikers. Coach the deputies and vigilantes on the law of unlawful assembly, inciting to riot, disorderly conduct, etc., so that, unhampered by any thought that the strikers may also possess some rights, they will be ready and anxious to use their newly acquired authority to the limit.

Fifth: And perhaps most important, heighten the demoralizing effect of the above measures—all designed to convince the strikers that their cause is hopeless—by a "back to work" movement, operated by a puppet association of so-called "loyal employees" secretly organized by the employer. Have this association wage a publicity campaign in its own name and coordinate such campaign with the work of the "missionaries" circulating among the strikers and visiting their homes. This "back to work" movement has these results: it causes the public to believe that the strikers are in the minority and that most of the employees desire to return to work. . . . This "back to work" movement also enables the employer, when the plant is later opened, to operate it with strike breakers if necessary and to continue to refuse to bargain collectively with the strikers. In addition, the "back to work" movement also enables the employer to keep a constant check on the strength of the union through the number of applications received from employees ready to break ranks and return to work. . . .

Sixth: When a sufficient number of applications are on

185

hand, fix a date for an opening of the plant through the device of having the opening requested by the "back to work" association. Together with the Citizens' Committee, prepare for such an opening by making provision for a peak army of police, by roping off the areas surrounding the plant, by securing arms and ammunitions, etc. The purpose of the "opening" of the plant is threefold: to see if the employees are ready to return to work; to induce still others to return as a result of the demoralizing effect produced by the opening of the plant and the return of some of their number; and lastly, even if the movement fails to induce a sufficient number of persons to return, to persuade the public through pictures and news releases that the opening was nevertheless successful.

Seventh: Stage the "opening," theatrically throwing open the gates at the propitious moment and having the employees march into the plant grounds in a massed group protected by squads of armed police. . . . Along with the "opening" provide a spectacle—speeches, flag-raising, and praises for employees, citizens, and local authorities, so that, their vanity touched, they will feel responsible for the continued success of the scheme.

Eighth: Capitalize on the demoralization of the strikers by continuing the show of police force and the pressure of the Citizens' Committee, both to insure that those employees who have returned will continue at work and to force the remaining strikers to capitulate. If necessary, turn the locality into a warlike camp through the declaration of a state of emergency tantamount to martial law, and barricade it from the outside world, so that nothing may interfere with the successful conclusion of the "Formula." . . .

Ninth: Close the publicity barrage, which day by day

186

during the entire period has increased the demoralization worked by all these measures, on the theme that the plant is in full operation and that the strikers were merely a minority attempting to interfere with "the right to work," thus inducing the public to place a moral stamp of approval upon the above measures. With this, the campaign is over—the employer has broken the strike.

There are several answers to this question of employer antipathy toward unionism. To begin with, he has the responsibility of making his concern show a profit. And to carry through this assignment he believes that he should have control over his "agents of production," be able to combine them, whether machines or buildings or human labor, into a profit-yielding undertaking. Like anyone else who bends his energies toward attaining a certain goal, he doesn't relish the prospect of "outside interference." And this attitude has been reinforced by the ingrained individualism of American character. It is also reinforced by the all too human impulse of the man wielding power to nourish and expand his ego by asserting his authority for the sheer pleasure of throwing his weight around. Many employers prefer paternalism, or benevolent tyranny, to trying out industrial democracy. They want the warm glow of feeling that they are charitable and "take care of" their employees rather than encouraging the latter to stand on their own feet. At the very moment such employers, through the Na-

tional Association of Manufacturers and the United
States Chamber of Commerce, are singing hosannas to
self-reliance, they are denying it to their workers by
prohibiting unionism, the only vehicle available to
them for attaining self-reliance and personal independence, since as individuals they are impotent.

In an industry where sharp competition is the rule,
the employer is under constant temptation to lower
costs by reducing wages, since among all the items of
overhead, labor is the least scarce and the most flexible. Hence he tends to feel that a union which almost
by instinct opposes wage-cuts destroys his influence
over costs, his ability to meet a rival's prices by this
means, his control over all factors making for success
or failure.

On the other hand, in an industry where monopolistic competition prevails, where prices are pegged,
rendered sticky or inflexible by agreements among
various firms, the sheer impersonality of the top officialdom produces the same results. In our thousand
largest corporations, for example, which are big and
integrated and under the sway of great financiers, decisions as to labor policy are laid down by directors
who are banking-minded rather than production-
minded. They tend to visualize the company more in
terms of balance sheets, charts, graphs, figures in a
row, and less in terms of people fusing many minds,
hands, talents to turn out a commodity. And whereas

188

it is easy enough to buy, move, or scrap the inanimate agents of wealth-creation and to balance them against the equally inanimate symbols of the counting-house, the handling of human beings who have their feelings, their aspirations, presents complications not so easily resolved.

Ever since 1919 American employers and their surrogates have been especially conscious of the need for closer contact between themselves and their workers. They perceived that a certain minimum of labor contentment was necessary to the smooth functioning of their enterprise. They have sought for some method of communication that would take the place of the direct personal contact of a bygone day. They saw that industry may grow tremendously without impairing their grasp over financing, marketing, producing; but that personnel problems tended to become more vexing and difficult with every extension in size. Straw-boss, foreman, supervisor, superintendent, plant manager failed to provide this communication, and for two reasons. First of all, men placed in charge of production are usually chosen for technical knowledge and proficiency. Few are either trained or adroit in personnel questions. Moreover, their bonuses and their promotions depend upon their ability to ensure profits. If a local manager raises his costs for the sake of the workers, his own job is in jeopardy.

During the past twenty years, moreover, the trend

toward mergers and consolidations has centralized control over both financial and operating policies of more than fifty per cent of industry in the hands of two thousand magnates. They are as a rule removed from the actual producing scene. They are inaccessible to the worker, yet their decrees are the laws governing his life. When the board of directors, for example, of a vast holding company with widely scattered plants decides to shut down one subsidiary or start up another, to cut wages, or to use machinery instead of human labor, it is reacting to the stimuli of cost sheets, reports from minor officials, clamor for dividends. They are not thinking about the people who make these dividends possible. Hence over the last two decades impersonality as against a sense of responsibility for steady employment, good wages, and decent working conditions has tended to dehumanize "capital-labor" relations.

And to remedy this defect, to help transform the worker from an anonymous badge or number into something like a human being, and at the same time to offset the appeals of any genuine unionism, employers often turned to various "company" unions and employee-representation schemes—many of them devised by personnel directors. At first many believed that these were going to be a solution. They featured stock-ownership plans, bonuses, group insurance, outings, picnics, baseball games among departmental teams,

190

and the like. But they had two vital defects. Their funds and their officials and their programs were provided by management. They were therefore an expression of paternalism rather than of self-help and self-reliance by the workers. And such company unions, or "councils," or "brotherhoods," or "associations," for their names were innumerable, could at best engage in collective consultation over minor points, not in collective bargaining over major issues. They could obtain hot running water for the men's washroom. They could do nothing to add to the bulge in the weekly pay-envelope. They had no treasury for a strike; no experts to press their claims. Their leaders who were on the company's pay-roll were often reluctant to transmit any complaints lest this very process testify to their failure in keeping members contented and confident that they were getting a square deal.

Finally, the company union was localized; it was confined to a single plant. As a genus it could not help to eliminate chiselers by doing its share to stabilize and standardize conditions on a national scale—services performed in coal, for instance, by the United Mine Workers and in women's wear by the International Ladies' Garment Workers.

From the passage of the National Labor Relations Act to the present, however, many employers including such giants as United States Steel, the American Woolen Mills, the Libbey-Owens-Ford Company, the

General Electric Corporation, and a long list of others belonging to what is often called the Blue Book of American industry have accepted collective bargaining with outside, independent, bona-fide unions. Together with hundreds of other firms, more or less prominent, they look upon it more and more as filling a need for maintaining orderly, organized industrial relations. They regard company unionism as outmoded, as having failed to accomplish this end.

Despite the intransigence of the Ford Motor Company and a number of others whose management lives mentally in covered-wagon days, it would be safe to assume that collective bargaining has come to stay—if it were not for the split in the labor movement and its repercussions.

Whereas the NLRB is concerned basically with removing causes of conflict between employer and unions, or workers who want to form them, events have thrust it into the hot-box of the AFL-CIO dispute. In its second fundamental function, that of determining the appropriate unit for collective bargaining, all the turmoil and bitterness, all the vexations and bickering generated by AFL-CIO warfare have been dumped in its lap, as if even without this added complication the task of administering Section 9 weren't arduous enough.

"The complexity of modern industry, transportation and communication," said the Board in its first annual report, "and the diverse forms which organization has taken among employees, precludes the application of rigid rules." This is a triumph of understatement. In order to ascertain the due and proper unit, the Board has had to fashion its own yardsticks, to invoke common sense, to study the history of labor organization within an industry, to survey the functional and geographic coherence of a particular corporation, to consider the type of work and the degree of skill required for its execution, and to examine the habits, customs, and preferences of the workers concerned. From this farrago, however, three broad examples may be cited as a guide to the Board's criteria.

When efforts were made to subdivide the workers of the Huth and James Shoe Company (Milwaukee) into eight different craft unions—namely, cutters, fitters, lasters, sole-leatherers, bottomers, finishers, wood-heelers, and packers—each to become a separate bargaining unit, the Board said "No." Rather it ruled that "since the shoe manufacturing industry today is virtually without craft unions," an industrial or plant-wide unit rather than the company's producing set-up, would be more "appropriate" and better serve the interests of the workers.

And, by the same token, in the *Matter of Marcus Loew Booking Agency* the Board declared that engineers comprised a unit apart from others employed at the company's broadcasting station. "The radio broadcast engineers," the Board said, "are technical employees engaged in work of a highly skilled nature, have qualifications and duties different from those of other employees, and are required to hold Federal licenses. . . . It requires years of study in a school for radio engineering, technical training of a distinctive type and some experience before one can procure such a license. Their salaries average about $50.00 a week. They work 8 hours a day and 6 days a week. Their interests are mutual and alike, and they have very little in common with other groups of employees. They constitute a distinct unit."

Similarly the Board mortised out the "little cigar" department of the American Tobacco Company's plant at Reidsville, North Carolina, from the main bargaining units of the workers there. "The little cigar department," the Board found, "is really a factory within a factory. It could as well be operated entirely independent of the rest of the Reidsville plant." It concluded therefore that the little-cigar operatives deserved a unit of their own.

Yet once it has gauged the appropriate unit, the Board then has to name the union to represent it. Methods for doing this vary. Sometimes the Board accepts proof of majority support for a given union when it is offered in the form of signed membership cards, union ledgers which list dues-paying adherents within the unit, the employer's acknowledgment that the union has a majority in his plant, and so on. But when a question arises as to whether union A or union B or none at all may be wanted to represent the workers, the Board "puts it up to the men themselves." It holds elections, often setting up tents as its voting booths. On the ballot the worker frequently makes his choice between an AFL union, a CIO union, an unaffiliated union, a company union, and "no union." And such elections are seemingly popular; for from 1937 forward more than ninety-six per cent of all workers eligible to vote (usually those who have been employed by the company over a minimum period) have actually cast their ballots; a fact that would seem once and for all to refute the frequent charge that workers are indifferent or apathetic to the fate of unionism in their own shop.

And to illustrate just how this works out in practice, consider a typical twelvemonth. In the 1,152 elections conducted by the Board for the fiscal year ending June 30, 1938, the AFL and CIO together won 816. Unaffiliated national unions, neither AFL nor CIO, won 45; local unions of the same type won 84. The number of contests lost by all forms of labor organizations was 207, including 13 tie votes. In any event, in cases where the workers want collective bargaining, the group that gets the most votes is certified by the Board as the bargaining agent.

Until 1939 the Board did not permit the employer to ask for an election. It was afraid that this might de-

195

feat the aims of the Act. It believed that some employers, knowing that a new union hadn't had time to enroll a majority of their workers, would call for an election in which the union would lose and its campaign be halted before it had fairly begun. The AFL-CIO schism, however, compelled the Board to revise this part of the procedure completely, granting to employers the right to petition for a ballot show-down at their pleasure, for they were obviously suffering inconvenience and hardship without recourse to that right. Time and again jurisdictional strikes between the AFL and the CIO forced cessation of operations, and literally tied up the works by "cross-picketing." In such cases the employer was an innocent bystander, injured by the belligerents and unable to do anything about it, since in these fights it often happened that neither the AFL nor the CIO was sure of a majority, and hence refused to ask for an election to decide the issue. Without this kind of request the Board was powerless to intervene.

In reversing itself on this question, and in permitting employers to ask for elections, the Board displayed an admirable amount of courage. After all, the AFL-CIO cleavage was nothing of the Board's making or choosing and has plagued it at every turn. Moreover, since organized labor has no final arbiter capable of settling the spectacular clashes between the AFL and the CIO, the Board has voluntarily shouldered this burden to the fullest possible extent. When the Board rules in an

AFL-CIO row, that ruling sticks; at least up until early 1940 neither AFL nor CIO has dared to challenge any of its decisions by further strikes or picketing, whatever the legal challenges by amendments launched against the Board's authority. It should be kept in mind that all these amendments have been inspired by the AFL-CIO fracas, and by such incidents as the following:

From 1936 to 1938 the CIO Longshoremen on the west coast were being built up from a nucleus which had withdrawn from the AFL and were attracting many new recruits. The CIO union, early in 1938, appealed to the Board to be certified as bargaining agent for the "longshore" industry along the Pacific. It pointed out that of the 12,860 Longshoremen on the Coast it had 9,557 or 74.3 per cent. In every port except four in the state of Washington it had a majority of workers. But in these four ports the rival AFL union was under contract with employers, and these agreements had been signed before the defection from the AFL of the groups forming the CIO union. The question was therefore raised as to whether in negotiations for the renewal of existing contracts, the CIO union should deal for the entire Coast or whether each union should deal for the ports in which it had a majority. The Board weighed the pros and cons of this delicate and symbolic issue for some time. It discovered that all the employers in this territory were bargaining by means of their own union, the Waterfront

197

Employers Association. The Board discovered also that a chief source of employer-employee discord was the unsatisfactory character of carrying on collective bargaining on a local basis, as in former days. From their experience, it appeared, employers had concluded that their own closely allied interests almost forced them to get together and co-operate. The Board, after prolonged study, inferred that effective bargaining on labor's side could also be most readily attained by that kind of alignment. In short, a "united front" of employers and a "united front" of Longshoremen existed, save for the AFL's four affiliates in the four Washington ports. The Board finally took the view that this valuable solidarity of the longshoremen was something that had comparatively little to do with the *economics* of collective bargaining, especially when based on the principle of majority rule. Wages, hours, and work-conditions were everywhere the same. Hence, it was said, in effect, that the minority of the four AFL unions reflected what was essentially the political and personal, rather than the economic, issue of the contest for power and place between AFL and CIO leaders. In this instance, continued the Board, such rivalries were extraneous to the fundamental problem of orderly, efficient handling of management-union relationships. In other words, the Board apparently reasoned that the relatively non-economic interests of the twenty-five per cent of the AFL

198

unions were secondary to the economic interests of all Longshoremen. It therefore named the CIO union as collective bargaining agent for the whole west coast.

And it was a consequence of this ruling that the AFL's attacks on the Board acquired a savage intensity. William Green and Daniel Tobin and other AFL spokesmen accused it of trampling on the rights of minorities, of favoring the CIO without rhyme or reason, for the sake of aiding the Federation's rival. And chief among the AFL's amendments to the Act is the provision to eliminate this discretionary power of the Board.

The AFL's proposed amendments, indeed, go even further. They would make it mandatory for the Board to certify in every instance a craft union—wherever and whenever it may exist, and its members may decide that they want to bargain collectively by themselves. What the Federation's leadership expects to gain from this formula is less justice for specially skilled groups than the Board's assistance in fighting the CIO by giving the Federation the right to invoke its own discretion in fashioning so-called craft unions to fit any situation that may suit its advantage. After all, when welders of the Ryan Aeronautical Company, in San Diego, wanted to set up a separate and distinct union of their own, the AFL affiliate in the plant, the International Association of Machinists, said: "Nothing doing." It claimed that the process of welding was not a craft; for the Machinists had organized the plant on an industrial basis. But in the Pittsburgh Dairy Products Company case, the AFL affiliate, the Bookkeepers and Accountants Union, sliced off eight cashiers from an office force of 123, and stated that this octet comprised a craft, of and by themselves. What the AFL is really aiming at is to have the Board automatically recognize any type of union structure that the Federation may find or imagine to be a craft. An industrial union, a trade union, or any other union can be christened a craft. Hence in any AFL-CIO contest the former's affiliate, on its craft name alone, will cross the tape the winner —by government edict in a fixed race.

Moreover, in its projected revisions of the Wagner Act, as embodied in the Walsh Bill S. 1000, the AFL has injected a very subtle and hazardous change into the meaning of the term "labor organization." Under the Act, as it now stands, the Board is of course empowered to determine whether or not any particular labor organization is company-controlled, whether the company has intervened in the formation, the policy, or the personnel of any union on its premises. The AFL, however, would apparently conjure up a very special and curious designation of a company union, and what it may do, and what the employer may do to it, with it, in it, and for it. The Federation has devised a plan by which legal evidence must be presented to show that the corporation, through its board of directors or other top management, has "created, dominated, maintained or controlled" a union. Otherwise, unless this fact can be definitely established, the union would be treated as legitimate, as coming under the normal and statutory classification of a "labor organization." But with this definition of a company union it is virtually impossible to prove the charge that the board of directors of any firm has participated in creating a company-run union. In automobiles, to be concrete, you would have to show definitely that Mr. Alfred P. Sloan, or others of the General Motors Corporation's ruling hierarchy, personally sponsored a company union. At best this logic displays a naïveté matched only by its self-destructive implications. Its practical effects are an open-season invitation to employers to foster company unions and conceal their methods of doing it. A foreman, a superintendent, a lawyer, a Harry Bennett, or a Father Coughlin all can be the intermediaries for building a company union of the most vicious kind without betraying the connection between the corporation's top-flight executives and their techniques of domination, and without ever falling athwart the law.

It may be kept in mind that this neo-Machiavellian strategy was inspired by the Board's custom of voiding what it deemed to be collusive contracts between the Federation and various business concerns. The ground on which the Board has invalidated such AFL pacts is perhaps best surveyed by an extract from testimony given by William Green before the Senate Committee

201

on Hearings on Amendments to the Wagner Act.

It appears that in the Tennessee Copper Company case the Board charged that the AFL had obtained the active aid of the firm's important supervisory officials, and that the company had therefore engaged in the "unfair labor practice" of influencing the selection of the appropriate collective bargaining unit for its employees.

The Board contended, for example, that Young Querry, assistant general foreman, had told a worker that if the CIO won the impending election, John L. Lewis would certainly call a "sympathetic strike." O. K. Lyle, general foreman, assured another worker that the CIO was un-American and subversive, and that if it emerged the victor, the whole plant would be closed down. Again, Martin Hanby, the general rigger foreman, informed a pro-CIO worker that "You better lay off that bunch there. The CIO ain't anything here." The superintendent of the Tennessee Copper Company, D. B. Epperson, advised employees to cast their ballots for the AFL, since Lewis was a dictator and if they voted for the CIO they might as well "kiss your jobs good-by."

On the basis of such evidence the Board tossed the AFL-Tennessee Copper contract into the ash-can and ordered a brand-new election, which the CIO won. When Mr. Green was questioned on the witness stand by Senator Ellender about all this monkey business, the president of the AFL found himself in something of a predicament.

"It is my information," said the Senator, "and I may be wrong about it, Mr. Green, that Mr. Epperson or . . . Mr. Hanby was the general foreman of an entire group? . . ."

Mr. Green: "Possessing the power to hire and discharge?"

Senator Ellender: "Well, I don't know about that, but another question I wanted to ask you was, why was it that you . . . agreed that these supervisory employees should not vote at the election to be held?"

Mr. Green: "I don't know that such an agreement was made, was it?"

Senator Ellender: "The record so shows, yes, sir. . . ."

Mr. Green: "*Well, the voters, the members of the union could not be influenced by anything that a foreman said, because they went into a booth and voted a secret ballot in accordance with their judgment and their experience. The mere statement that was made by someone could not be accepted as sufficient ground to invalidate. That is the point I am asking.*" (Italics mine.)

Senator Ellender: "Of course, you know good and well that it would be rather a difficult matter to prove that the head of a company or any members on its Board directly influenced workers?"

203

Mr. Green: "But it ought to be proven before you set aside a contract. You shouldn't jump at conclusions."

Senator Ellender: "But I am wondering what influence it would have on the Board if it is shown that a foreman who has charge of a whole group of persons in one factory—wouldn't that lead you . . . to believe that whatever that foreman did, having so many people under his jurisdiction, would it not lead you to believe that probably he was—"

Mr. Green (interrupting): "*Not so necessarily, because a large number of our members resent bitterly any suggestion on the part of the company through anybody, and when they go into the booth and vote their sentiments, they had that resentment in mind. . . .*" (Italics mine.)

It would seem obvious enough that in this fooling around with employer collusion the AFL is pursuing a course that lays labor's head neatly and firmly under the guillotine of an employer control that unionism by its nature must avoid; and that in thus trying to plague the CIO, the Federation not only is forging instruments to impede the progress of its competitor but also is lighting the funeral pyre for its own immolation. To offset this AFL brand of employer-union collusion, the CIO has urged in its own proposed amendments to the Wagner Act that criminal penalties be inflicted upon enterprises which violate any of its provisions. And to stymie the AFL's new accent on "craft anywhere and

204

any time," the CIO would alter the Act to prevent what it has described as "carving-up operations" on the body of industrial unions, the turning of "big ones into little ones." In short, the antithetical approach toward the Wagner Act on the part of the AFL and the CIO not only stems from their schism but now has vested interests and vested emotions of its own. When the AFL assails the Board as "dictatorial" and the CIO advises only a "sparing and moderate" use of the Act, and when both accuse the Board of bias toward their rival, they provide the opponents of the whole idea of government aid to unionism with their clinching argument.

"Obviously," they now say, in effect, "the whole Labor Board set-up is unfair and prejudiced—even labor, both sides of labor, admits it. Just look at the record. The AFL wants to change the Act and has been successful in getting rid of that fellow Smith, the other Smith, on the Board. The CIO also wants to change the Act and is dissatisfied with the Board's personnel and would like to see Leiserson dumped. And there you are!"

The attacks upon the Board by both the AFL and the CIO have immensely heartened the foes of collective bargaining. Under the pretense of making the Act "fair," and to take advantage of the confusion about its purposes—a confusion to which the AFL and the CIO have contributed more than their share—the National Association of Manufacturers and kindred sodalities have put forward a lengthy list of amendments to obscure the real issues. They recommend, for example, that the Act be revised so that an employee will not be subject to "coercion" from any source, and then tie in a subsection whereby a union organizer's "sales-talk" becomes "coercion." They suggest that a union which has been "guilty of violence" in any form shall forfeit its right to be recognized by the employer; and thus open the back door for all the abuses of American employers in "planting" or provoking acts of violence and then blaming the union for them. They would redefine the word "employee" to exclude all "agricultural" workers, meaning those in canneries, sawmills, and even meat-processing plants. All such amendments, of course, are designed to defeat the Act's aims and are extraneous to the Board's actual functioning. Naturally, an Act which seeks to advance unionism will protect the right of a union organizer to peddle his wares. To ask the Board to mete out punishment for acts of violence is the same as asking it to prevent burglary. Such things are, of course, in the province of local police authorities. To deprive workers who handle the products of the soil in any way of the Act's protection of their right to bargain collectively is a transparent subterfuge to insert the practice of group exclusion. Yet, aided by the nation's press, which, as a whole, has written its most thoroughly underhanded and contemptible chapter in its spotlighting of anything "bad" about the

Board, in its embellishing of any failures, and its playing down of the Board's solid, magnificent achievements, those who would geld unionism stand an excellent chance within the next year or two of clipping and chiseling away at the Act until it is utterly emasculated, until the Board becomes merely a decorative body. In that direction, of course, lie the restoration of the open-shop, the "American plan," and other devices for assuring the complete ascendancy of the employer and the equally complete subjugation of the worker. Without the political and economic might of a strong united labor movement, this trend is something that the perennial optimists who lead the AFL and the CIO might well ponder; the more especially since the "revelations" of the Smith Committee investigating the NLRB have teased up and amplified anti-union attitudes among both employers and the public at large.

Despite the Smith Committee's disclosures that a number of the Board's examiners and the like are arrogant, fresh-from-law-school people, very wet behind the ears, and with a sophomore's contempt for the amenities, and despite the undue front-page scare headlines given to such flaws in personnel, nobody has been able to unearth any citations to show that the Board has been essentially biased in favor of either the AFL or the CIO. On the whole, the record reveals that the AFL has had a slight edge over the CIO, winning in 262 polls as against its rival's score of 260, for the fiscal year ending

June 30, 1939. Moreover, in the 48 most important test cases reflecting the AFL-CIO conflict over the past four years, the CIO won 24, the AFL 22, with two ties.

Since the Wagner Act was passed in 1935 the total of union membership in the United States, exclusive of railroad workers, who come under the purview of the National Mediation Board, has risen from three million to about eight and one half million. Moreover, since early 1938 and throughout 1939 the number of man-days of idleness caused by strikes has dropped from three and a half million to less than two million; and this downward trend would have been vastly accentuated were it not for AFL-CIO jurisdictional disputes, and their picketing of each other. Up to the present time the Board has won twelve out of sixteen decisions in tests before the United States Supreme Court. It has handled up to date 22,402 cases, covering 4,501,749 workers, disposing of them as follows:

50 per cent, or 11,121 cases, involving 1,874,345 workers, were closed by agreement, satisfying both employer and employees;

27 per cent, or 6,053 cases, covering 1,165,363 workers, were withdrawn, the employer winning;

16 per cent, or 3,611 cases, covering 877,555 workers, were dismissed, the employer winning;

7 per cent, or 1,617 cases, covering 584,486 workers, went to final trial and decision, with the workers winning 66 2-3 per cent and the employers winning 33 1-3 per cent.

And all this surely is a record that should revive a flagging faith in the adaptability of the democratic process, in the slow, steady pull toward greater social and economic equality by day-to-day adjustments, as against the specious celerity of totalitarian heroics. Yet instead of assisting the Act to become the self-repealing measure it should be, as the Board helps to transform industry's adolescent labor policy into maturity, the AFL and the CIO, for their own parochial reasons, still are undermining the prestige of the Act and the Board alike. More than any other factor, the AFL-CIO warfare has deflected, if not subverted, the purposes of the Act, created suspicion of its administrators, confused the public mind, and shaken the foundations of a reform long overdue, which by now should have been firmly, rather than precariously, established.

CHAPTER VII

MENE, MENE, TEKEL, UPHARSIN

WHILE IN Washington, D. C., the AFL and the CIO were busy fighting each other to put over their mutually opposed views of what should be done to the Wagner Act, anti-union forces in other parts of the country, quick to seize the advantages given them by labor's split, were blowing up collective-bargaining defenses, state by state, with blitzkrieg audacity.

On a wet, dreary Tuesday in November 1938 the citizens of Oregon passed by 197,000 to 146,500 votes the most vicious and barbaric anti-labor measure in the legislative history of the United States. It is still on the books. A state Supreme Court decision has upheld its constitutionality. Many able lawyers expect that when a final "test" case on this statute reaches the United States Supreme Court, that tribunal may also pronounce it valid—on the double ground that it was passed as a referendum and therefore directly reflects the will of the people, and that states, as still somewhat sovereign commonwealths, should be allowed wide latitude in legislative experiments occurring within their own borders.

In any event "it" has happened in Oregon so far as labor is concerned. And it happened, as in the past, and as in the future it will continue to happen, because John L. Lewis was too busy playing pat-a-cake with grandeur and William Green was too busy pumping platitudes at the ghost of Gompers to attend to the question of safeguarding union rights in the only way they can be safeguarded in these troubled times, by united action on the part of all organized labor.

The curtain on this labor tragedy was first raised in 1936, when twenty-odd thousand lumber, sawmill, furniture, and veneer workers in the Northwest seceded from the AFL United Brotherhood of Carpenters and Joiners and formed a rival International Woodworkers' Union, which was chartered by the CIO in July 1937. In retaliation Big Bill Hutcheson, head of the Carpenters and chairman of the Republican Labor Committee, instructed all members of his union not to handle "CIO wood." And to make this boycott more effective he also persuaded Dave Beck, overlord of the Teamsters on the west coast, and a puissant figure politically, to prevent his people from hauling or trucking or loading or storing this CIO wood. And soon squads of AFL pickets, equipped with rubber stamps and pads, were surrounding Oregon mills where the CIO had been recognized and affixing the *verboten* sign on all CIO-contaminated products they were able to lay hands on. And within three months, from August 15 to December 15, this boycott had forced eight sawmills around Portland to close down. And within the same twelve-week period losses in the lumber industry in the Columbia River Basin alone exceeded nine million dollars. In the forests of this region no trees crashed. In the planing mills no saws whirred. In the furniture factories flybelts were silent and wheels slowed to a stop.

Employers such as H. B. Van Dusen, president of the pro-union Inman-Poulsen mill, let it be known that they were willing and eager to revise existing contracts with CIO unions, or to sign new contracts with AFL unions, if only they had somebody with whom they could deal, if only they could get men back to work. But neither the AFL nor the CIO would permit this to be amicably accomplished. Instead, they kept picketing each other while orders were being lost, wages were not being paid, and paralysis ensued.

Ax-handle rows between AFL Carpenters and Teamsters and CIO Woodworkers sent more than nine hundred men to the hospital for treatment of injuries ranging from concussion to laceration. In saloons and streets jagged beer-bottle fights were epidemic. Despite the appeals and advice of various ministers, journalists, teachers, and others who didn't want to see labor literally giving itself a black eye, the AFL Central Labor Council in Portland asserted on December 8, 1937: "The boycott of CIO lumber will be continued and intensified. Any mill which attempts to operate CIO will face this boycott. Mills which resume operations with AFL employees will be aided in finding a market for their products."

As the Christmas season approached its climax, retailers were in despair. Sales were dipping, holiday stocks remained on the shelves, and the extension of credit to strikers on both sides by grocers, butchers, clothing merchants, druggists was reaching the saturation point. The city of Portland, where the lumber industry accounts for forty-five cents out of every pay-roll dollar, staggered under a relief burden that sent local taxes up while business reached a standstill and unemployment rose.

Yet in face of this virtual collapse of an important industry, Hutcheson and his Carpenters were adamant. So was Dave Beck. And so was Harold J. Pritchett, leader of the Woodworkers. Nor was the situation helped by the AFL charge that Pritchett, Canadian-born, and an intimate of Harry Bridges, was an alien and a suspected Communist. In return, the CIO charged that Dave Beck and his adherents were out-

213

and-out racketeers. "Red-racketeer—racketeer-Red." The chant continued until early in 1938 the Woodworkers, outnumbered and outgeneraled, were forced into submission. They quit the CIO union, by the thousand. They joined the AFL union. It was conceded that the Federation had emerged the victor. Many new AFL contracts appeared throughout the lumber industry, which, after losing millions in markets and goodwill, began to revive. But it was a Pyrrhic victory. The people of Oregon were outraged. Thousands of them directly, and other thousands indirectly, had been financially injured by the repercussions of this senseless war. They were smarting under the "public be damned" character of the AFL-CIO dispute. They were convinced that "labor had overplayed its hand." When the initiative designed to hamstring all union activity, legitimate as well as internecine, was presented to them they passed it, a fact which in itself was a minor revolution in a state which has been "liberal" in the best American tradition for fifty years. Yet this bill was passed with a preponderant number of votes coming from industrial districts where the wives of workers who had been victimized by this insensately imbecilic conflict conducted an extremely effective anti-union campaign of their own.

When the initiative was being proposed, the AFL suddenly awakened with a shock. Dave Beck blanched. He was up against something the strong-arm tactics of his own goon-squads, or his "little New Deal" arrangements with employers to maintain prices, couldn't beat down. Pritchett was equally frightened, and equally inept.

A new organization, a masquerade of Big Business, was sponsoring this union-muzzling measure, and doing it with a skill and smartness in public relations that left both Beck and Pritchett dazed and bumbling in bewilderment. Despite the danger signals, however, both the AFL and the CIO were too frenzied in their favorite pursuit of knifing each other to get together effectually and ward off the attacks of this common foe. There were, to be sure, some last-minute, fatuous efforts to launch a counter-attack against the Associated Farmers' cry of "support the farmers' measure, vote for initiative 316-X, turn apathy into action, get behind this anti-racket bill of your 65,000 farmers, make labor responsible." The AFL and the CIO together collected a paltry ten thousand dollars with which to combat a campaign that threatened their very existence and that, by means of billboards, handbills, newspaper advertisements, radio programs, and flying squadrons of sound-truck speakers, cost anywhere from four to fourteen times that much.

The result has been that union gains, achieved slowly, step by step over the past half-century, have melted away in Oregon like butter in the sun. Loggers in the pine forests, stevedores along the waterfront,

215

weavers in the knitting mills, tuna fishermen in the Pacific, all labor in the state, have taken wage-cut after wage-cut, without resistance. They cannot resist. Picket lines vanish under the slightest threat of an injunction. Under the provisions of this incredible Oregon law no strike is legal unless it embraces an absolute majority of workers in a given establishment. Hence if the employees of a chain-store branch in Oregon wanted to go on strike they would first have to get all the other employees of the chain in all other states to go on strike with them. Clerks and other workers in an A & P store in Oregon cannot withdraw their labor-power unless more than fifty per cent of the clerks and other workers of all A & P stores in the United States signify their intention of doing the same thing. While this may seem utterly fantastic, it is exactly the way the law is being interpreted.

Craft-type unions are especially hard hit under this statute. They usually comprise only a portion of the labor force; and thus in a small factory of a hundred employees, ten of them machinists, the machinists cannot go on strike unless they can persuade the other ninety workers to join them. All jurisdictional strikes, of course, are completely banned. Hence an employer can recognize one per cent of his workers as a company union. Then if the other ninety-nine per cent of his employees should go on strike against him, it would be a "jurisdictional" question, a war between rival "unions,"

216

and consequently the action of the majority would be illegal. The law likewise forbids any strike over union recognition. All boycotts, direct and indirect, are rigorously eliminated. Unions cannot publish "unfair to organized labor" lists. They may collect funds only for "legitimate requirements" and it is up to the courts to determine what these requirements may be. Already this has by implication thwarted union contributions for political purposes. No individual may be "hindered" from selling his labor to any enterprise that may wish to hire him. This makes it a crime even to shout "scab" at a Chowderhead Cohn. All "coercion"—in short, any organizer's conversation—in soliciting union membership is also banned. More than one hundred collective-bargaining agreements in Oregon and California were formally destroyed two months after the passage of initiative 316-X, and more than half of all others are being ignored or chiseled at informally.

At the same time such protective labor legislation as the Norris-LaGuardia Anti-Injunction Act, and the Wagner Act are virtually non-existent in Oregon; attempts to enforce their provisions are summarily brushed aside.

Meantime, the Associated Farmers has been going to town, and in swing time. It is a symbol and a storm-warning not only to organized labor but also to all who hold to the naïve belief that the democratic state can be maintained by repeating in solemn and sacerdotal tones

Washington's First Inaugural Speech and the Gettysburg Address. The Associated Farmers comprises a case study in totalitarian tactics. Even in adopting its name, it has taken a leaf from Hitler's book, that people will believe any lie if you repeat it often enough, and if it's a big lie, the better. The Associated Farmers is financed and directed by such honest sons of the soil as the Bank of America (owning more than fifty per cent of all farm lands in central and northern California); the Pacific Gas and Electric Company; the Southern Pacific Railroad; the California Packing Corporation; the Canners' League of California; the Spreckels Sugar Company; and the Industrial Association of San Francisco, the last among the most reactionary employers' groups in the United States.

The officers behind the canneries which put up apricots and oranges, the railroads which transport thousands of carloads of the land's produce, the light corporation supplying water and power for irrigation, could hardly tell a genuine farmer from a fairy. But to obscure their real objective of destroying unionism wherever it lifts its head, they have fashioned as window-dressing the figure who in the national consciousness is the typical American. He is the man who operates a "family-sized" farm, for a "living" rather than for "an actual or potential modern fortune," where he and his sons perform the sowing and the reaping, where hired help is the exception rather than the rule. The

Associated Farmers, on the other hand, was started in California in 1934 to keep migratory labor in the orchards and cotton lands in the hopeless and desperate peonage described with such excessive moderation by John Steinbeck in *The Grapes of Wrath*. The Associated Farmers, representing the great holdings where a farm or ranch is 15,000 acres and employs as many as 35,000 "hired hands," enacted anti-picketing "emergency" ordinances which enabled giant corporations to deputize their own agents to shoot at workers whenever they asked for a few pennies more than their subsubsistence wage-scale. It has caused workers' camps to be bombed and raided. It has ridden strike-leaders on rails and tarred and feathered them. It has published the most scurrilous anti-Semitic literature to see the light in this country over the past twenty-five years. It has faked dynamite and arson plots and blamed "union agitators" for them. It has lured Americans from Texas and Arkansas and Oklahoma, placed them in concentration camps, guarded by machine-guns, and kept them in a condition of servitude far more dreadful than that of Negroes on plantations in the South before the Civil War. It has opposed attempts to unionize the 250,000 workers in one of the nation's richest and most profitable industries by a reign of terrorism that makes Heinrich Himmler seem a bungling amateur. When on April 24, 1937 the Stockton Food Products Company was struck, Colonel W. E. Garrison, presi-

219

dent of the Associated Farmers, supplanted Sheriff Odell and directed the military maneuver of pouring round after round of tear-gas bombs into the ranks of unarmed and totally peaceful pickets, and then followed this oblation to the gods of law and order by volleys of buckshot that injured fifty strikers, according to reports of California's Commissioner of Immigration and Housing. Yet when the Governor sought to mediate this strike, the spokesman for the California Processors and Growers Association told him to keep his hands off, and he did with alacrity. For while the Associated Farmers conducted the immediate foray against workers asking for a fifty-cent-a-week raise, behind them was the transcendent might of the California Processors and Growers, and behind *them* was Libby, McNeill and Libby; the H. J. Heinz Corporation; the Barron-Packing Company, and similar concerns who liked what the Associated Farmers were doing and wanted more of it in what Carey McWilliams has aptly called "Factories in the Field." The farms, the purity of which the Associated Farmers are "protecting" from unionism worse than death, are industrial in pattern, not agrarian. They are vast ventures with interests ramifying from the west coast to banking and manufacturing spheres in other parts of the country. Certainly the leaders of the Associated Farmers are seemingly far more aware than either the AFL or the CIO chieftains that the chain of unionism is only as strong as its weakest link.

Hence the Associated Farmers has not confined its activity to agricultural labor, but is now extending it to include the Teamsters and the Longshoremen, the Garment Workers and the Carpenters, everyone in fact who carries a union card. At the same time it put over its initiative in Oregon, capitalizing on the public antagonisms aroused by the AFL-CIO feud, it sponsored similar measures in Washington and California—measures which were narrowly defeated. It should be kept in mind that the Associated Farmers is not merely another manifestation of local vigilantism of the older American tradition, although it displays all of its most vicious characteristics. The Dies Committee last year published a letter in which George Deatherage of the Knights of the White Camelia suggested that when General Moseley should begin his national Fascist movement, it should by all means include "Garrison of the Associated Farmers" as a man "on our side of the fence." John J. Phillips, its chief mouthpiece, declared in a speech on January 18, 1938 that "Hitler has done more for democracy than any man before him." Herman Cottrell, an Associated Farmers officer who helped to organize the union-busting California Cavaliers, has stated flatly: "We aren't going to stand for any more of these [union] organizers from now on; anyone who peeps about higher wages will wish he hadn't." And to promote this general point of view, the Associated Farmers very consciously considers itself a nucleus for a nation-wide movement to curb unions, and to ensure a national labor supply politically disfranchised and economically subservient. To attain this goal it has fostered various Agricultural Councils and Committees, quite as fraudulent as its own organization, pretending to represent the ordinary farmer, in five other states. Moreover, the Wisconsin Employment Peace Act, the very phrasing of which is a provocation to industrial discord, has been modeled directly upon the Oregon initiative 316-X. So have the slightly more moderate Minnesota and Michigan laws dealing with labor disputes. In Idaho last year a statute almost identical with 316-X was defeated only by gubernatorial veto. In South Carolina in the fall of 1940 the state legislature will pass upon a proposal which, in addition to embodying the essential features of the Oregon law, will force unions to contribute fifty per cent of their gross income directly to the state treasury. In Pennsylvania, Republican Governor Arthur H. James in signing amendments, in part "Oregon-inspired," which transformed the Keystone State's Little Wagner Act into a sword of Damocles over labor's head declared: "What we have done . . . is exactly what hundreds of people are telling Congress would be for the benefit of the nation."

From the autumn of 1938 forward, twenty-two of the forty-eight state legislatures in session during the past two years have either approved or debated or weighed

222

similar laws designed to hamstring unions, to render them "harmless."

Yet despite this handwriting on the wall, neither the AFL nor the CIO has displayed intelligence or vigor in combating the Associated Farmers and the legislative caponizing of unionism, and all that these portend. To be sure, after the horse was stolen in Oregon, both AFL and CIO lawyers locked the barn door; at least they plastered it with briefs. But before and during the theft they were too occupied with trying to harm each other to devote time to fending off the attacks of the present-day spearhead of a domestic Fascism that would destroy them both.

Despite the arduous efforts of President Roosevelt personally, and of his various ambassadors, to devise peace terms acceptable to the AFL-CIO belligerents, just two official unity conferences have been held during the four years of labor's warfare and these served only to intensify hostilities. The first began on October 25, 1937, at the Hotel Willard in Washington, D. C., in response to a CIO suggestion that meetings be held looking toward a "unified labor movement." At that time the AFL was glad to accept this idea, for it had been watching the CIO with considerable alarm, and the Federation's shogunate was appalled by the way applications for CIO membership had been swamping the CIO local office facilities, and by headlines heralding triumph after triumph for John L. Lewis & Company. Simultaneously, various CIO chieftains had been convinced by the late Charles P. Howard that the day had come to return to the AFL and capture it for the industrial-union principle.

At this conference the CIO, represented by a committee of ten, headed by Philip Murray, opened discussion with a proposal devised by Father Haas, of Catholic University, and the Roosevelt administration's chief nuncio in its attempts to close the AFL-CIO gap. The Haas plan called for the creation within the AFL of a separate autonomous branch to be known as the "CIO Department" and to embrace all of its affiliates. Moreover, the CIO wanted the Federation to guarantee that the industrial form of unionization would be accepted as "normal and necessary" in the mass-production, public-utility, marine, and basic fabricating industries, something that the AFL-CIO competition was doing in any case. The CIO also asked the AFL to amend its constitution to prevent, once and for all, the Executive Council from suspending any national or international union except by authority of a two-thirds majority vote in the annual convention.

The AFL committee of three, with Matthew Woll as chairman, at once discarded the Haas approach as impossible and unrealistic. They claimed that the proposed new CIO Department, with its craft, trade, semi-industrial, and industrial unions, would come into head-on collision with AFL unions in the same fields, and would thus simply aggravate, rather than allay, the jitters of jurisdiction.

After an interminable jockeying for position, the conferees finally rolled up their sleeves, took up pads and pencils, and got down to brass tacks. And at long last the AFL committee made a number of important concessions which, as embodied in its final offer, led most of those present to believe that a basis for agreement had been reached. It must be kept in mind that at this period in its development the CIO was composed of thirty-two unions. Seven of them had been ejected from the AFL, five had withdrawn, and the twenty others either had been created by the CIO itself or had affiliated with it after having previously enjoyed an independent status.

"Now, here's what we'll do," said the AFL committee, in effect. "The twelve original AFL unions don't need to come back into the Federation until all questions relating to the twenty new CIO affiliates have been ironed out by committees equally representing both sides. When such adjustments have been made, the new membership of the CIO will be taken back into the Federation *concurrently* with the twelve former CIO unions, and the CIO as such will cease to exist.

"When all such matters of readmission have been settled," continued the AFL spokesman, "we will recommend that our constitution be changed as the CIO suggests. We will also specify trade areas where the industrial form of organization shall entirely prevail."

Although minimized by CIO partisans and magnified by AFL spokesmen, the significance of these concessions can hardly be overestimated. For the twelve unions which had previously belonged to the AFL, and which had been on the whole enlarged under the CIO's ægis, comprised more than seventy-five per cent of the latter's numerical and financial strength; viz.:

United Mine Workers	550,000
Amalgamated Association of Iron, Tin and Steel Workers (SWOC)	375,000
United Automobile Workers	325,000
Textile Workers' Union (TWOC)	300,000
International Ladies' Garment Workers	250,000
Amalgamated Clothing Workers	225,000
Oil, Field, Gas Well and Refinery Workers	65,000
United Rubber Workers	60,000
Mine, Mill and Smelter Workers	50,000
International Fur Workers	40,000
American Newspaper Guild	17,000
Marine and Shipbuilding Workers	15,000[1]

There was surprisingly little trouble about the tentative reabsorption of this bloc into the AFL, although jurisdictional rights in some sections of the steel industry were fiercely debated. More genuine elements

[1] The International Typographical Union and the Cap and Millinery Workers Union were allied with the CIO only through their respective presidents, Charles P. Howard and Max Zaritsky, not through formal affiliation of their memberships.

226

of conflict existed between the AFL Carpenters and the CIO Woodworkers, for example, and the AFL Street Railway Employees and the CIO Transport Workers, the AFL's Electrical Workers and the CIO Radio, Machine and Electrical Workers. Still other unions, however, like the Newspaper Guild, had virtually no hurdles of jurisdiction to overcome.

Early in December 1937 the conference suddenly blew up, and special subcommittees, headed personally by Lewis and Green, were unable to salvage the pieces. The AFL version is that the first CIO committee had definitely accepted the Federation's formula, but that Lewis "vetoed" the entire agreement at the last minute. The CIO has contended, with some variations, that the AFL committee refused to put its terms in writing, that it lacked final authority to "sign, seal, and deliver," and that it wanted the CIO to abandon its newer affiliates. In any event, what with confusion and counter-charges, the story was given out that the issue was "ten inside, and twenty outside"; that is, the Federation would take back ten of the CIO unions and leave the twenty-two others out in the cold, to perish of neglect or fall prey to the jurisdictional wolves. In the first place, the ratio was twelve and twenty, and in the second place this wasn't the issue, a fact verified by the CIO's Philip Murray in a speech in New York City on January 5, 1938 when he declared: "Mr. Green has suggested, 'Well, you CIO men and your thirty-two unions stay

227

out of the Federation for a while. Appoint your committees, and we won't ask you to come in until everybody comes in.' "

Actually, the CIO had three basic demands: adoption of industrial-union practices in specified areas, the lifting of suspensions by the Executive Council, and the curtailing of its power to revoke charters. All these were substantially granted by the AFL, which in turn clung to its own single basic demand: the abolition of the CIO as a separate, "dual" entity.

In labor circles the consensus of informed opinion, even among certain CIO leaders, is that Lewis himself was primarily responsible for breaking off the 1937 negotiations, and that in doing so he missed the opportunity of a lifetime. After all, it is pointed out, in the November 1935 convention which resulted in labor's great divide, the CIO faction with its allies was able to count on more than a million out of three million workers. And by way of contrast and comparison, it is also pointed out, the AFL at its 1937 Denver convention listed 2,500,000 unionists, while the CIO—from the time of its creation to that of the Hotel Willard negotiations —had enrolled at least 3,200,000 and claimed even more. Hence, even granting it the short end of the trades and compromises needed for any merger, the CIO stood a better than even chance of going back to the Federation, where it still had many friends, notably among the Brewery Workers, the Hatters, the Bakers, and the Typographers, and of becoming within a year the dominant voice in shaping and executing the policy of the reunited body.

Moreover, the CIO was in late 1937 in a far stronger bargaining position for arranging any truce than it has subsequently enjoyed. From 1938 forward it was hard hit by three circumstances, causing it to recede from its high-water mark of the previous year. The recession during 1938 threw many thousands of CIO adherents out of work and made them unable to pay dues; the more especially since the mass-production groups which form most of the CIO's membership find it more difficult to obtain "fill-in" jobs than the AFL unionists, on the whole. For one thing, a machinist, when laid off in an automobile assembly plant, can usually pick up some fairly steady employment in a machine shop and the like until the slack season, or slack times in general, are over. Then, too, WPA, PWA, FSHA funds are largely spent in construction of parks and playgrounds, buildings, swimming-pools, roads. Thus the AFL Plumbers, Carpenters, Electricians, Caulkers, to say nothing of the Teamsters who drive the trucks, are needed for such projects, if only on a part-time basis. Indeed, the CIO treasury over the past three and one half years has reliably mirrored the ups and downs of the mass-production cycle, and in 1938 the CIO's income fell off appreciably, despite its ability to maintain union rates for its members still employed. Its ambitious program therefore was temporarily checked for lack of money.

At the same time Stalinist disruption provoked the withdrawal of such promising affiliates as the Southern Tenant Farmers Union, which wanted to help the share-croppers rather than help Donald Henderson, chief Stalinist organizer in the field of agricultural labor, dis-seminate pro-Soviet views. And in at least fifteen other CIO unions Stalinist "rule or ruin" tactics and diver-sion of union receipts and energies to party purposes resulted in internal bickerings, fist-fights, loss of faith in the CIO, and resignations that depleted its ranks by from ten to fifteen per cent.

Finally, when in the spring of 1938 the CIO let it be known that it intended to establish itself officially, and perhaps forever, as a national permanent organization rivaling the AFL, the CIO lost one of its richest, most progressive, and valuable affiliates: the International Ladies' Garment Workers. The leaders of this union, notably David Dubinsky, its president, had been the CIO's principal proponents of unity with the Federa-tion, waving the olive branch on every possible occa-sion, while contributing more than half a million dollars to the CIO organizing drives, and consistently support-ing the industrial-union principle. They warned the CIO against taking a step which would magnify, rather than subdue, the conflict with the Federation; and when their warning went unheeded, they and their followers withdrew from the CIO, primarily in order to keep pressing for labor peace.

Meantime the AFL—reinvigorated by CIO competition, and profiting immensely from the "I want to join a union" enthusiasm generated by CIO energy and daring—had passed its 1920 peak of more than four million members, and had so completely submerged the craft-industrial debate that it was chartering industrial unions with the same élan that marked the CIO chartering of craft unions.

When, therefore, in March 1939, President Roosevelt urged the AFL and the CIO to make another effort to get together, everybody understood that the real point at issue was no longer craft versus industrial organization, but rather the discovery of a satisfactory method for redistributing powers, prerogatives, and prestige among the individuals most directly concerned.

Both AFL and CIO acceded promptly to the President's request. But as soon as peace committees from both camps had met with Mr. Roosevelt in the White House and had received his benediction, John L. Lewis set off his unexpected and startling "One Big Union for Three" fireworks, with flare-headline effects. He urged that the AFL and the CIO dissolve forthwith, and that the "Big Four" Railroad Brotherhoods also disband, and that all three groups be merged into a new Congress of American Labor, the presidency of which was to go to an "executive type" such as A. F. Whitney of

231

the Trainmen or D. B. Robertson of the Firemen and Enginemen. He also proposed that for the first year of his new triple alliance the "services of the United States Department of Labor and its conciliation bureau shall be . . . available for cooperative mediation on all controversial questions affecting overlapping jurisdiction or other matters."

In some quarters it was believed that Lewis offered this solution in an earnest desire to reconcile differences. Most insiders, however, looked upon it at best as an indulgence in dubiously Homeric comedy, and at worst as an attempt to stall around in a critical situation, even a crisis. The AFL rejected the Lewis plan summarily as "not designed for serious consideration," and this description would seem correct enough.

On paper, of course, and in the future, some such grand combination of all union forces as suggested by Lewis might become not only desirable but mandatory. But at the time, it was—and remains—plain nonsense. The Big Four as a group are older even than the AFL. They operate within the framework of an industry that since 1888 has been directly regulated by the national government. They have their own traditions, customs, loyalties, a whole institutional complex at once ingrained and indigenous. Their collective-bargaining status is the result of a long, step-by-step evolution and experiment to meet the special conditions of "working on the railroad." To scrap this set-up by a

232

stroke of the pen would in itself create vast new problems—administrative, legislative, and jurisdictional—
and would needlessly complicate a condition already
sufficiently complex. And certainly Lewis's notion that
the final say-so in his projected Congress of American
Labor be vested in the Department of Labor is an extremely dangerous fooling with the concept of trans-
ferring the "direction of the labor movement from its
own hands into those of government officials," as the
AFL properly and quickly pointed out.

Despite Lewis's exhibition of what both AFL and
CIO spokesmen denounced as "clowning," the negotiations were resumed, even if with a somewhat dampened
ardor on both sides. And the AFL, prompted by
Green's pledge to the President that the Federation
would do everything it could to get peace, gave ground
on another point, carrying the concessions it had made
in the fall of 1937 a step further.

From 1936 forward, in building their national organizations, several CIO unions had extended their juris-
dictions. The United Mine Workers, for example, were
drawing in chemical workers, and the Amalgamated
Clothing Workers had invaded the laundry field. In an
earlier day the AFL would have objected strenuously
to this sort of thing as violating at least the paper claims
of various affiliates. But now it told such CIO unions
to return "as you are, not as you were."

The AFL insisted, however, that in any reunited body

233

representation would have to be based upon dues-paying membership. In other words, said the AFL conferees, votes, which mean influence in annual conventions, and in electing officers, must be allotted solely on the basis of so many votes for so many adherents who are in good standing—that is, who have paid up their regular and special assessments. "Bring your auditors and your books," said the AFL to the CIO, "and we'll bring ours, and we both will call in some impartial accountants from the outside, and then let's see, and we'll talk turkey."

It was at this juncture that the negotiations for all practical purposes began to break up. The CIO knew that in accord with this accountancy principle the AFL would have controlled the merged movement. Unlike the Federation, the CIO exonerates its members from paying dues "when unemployed due to strike, lockout or other involuntary cause." Hence in the spring of 1939, as now, the CIO had many thousands who were considered in good standing and were allowed to vote in their own organization, yet who had more enthusiasm than cash. Moreover, the CIO—what with unemployment in its chief industrial sectors, Stalinist machinations, the defection of the ILGWU, and the inexperiences of many of its newer unions—had declined from its spring of 1937 peak of 4,000,000 members to a (claimed) registration of 3,790,000. Less than 2,000,-000 of these were dues-paying unionists, while the AFL had, and still retains, twice that many.

On April 4, 1939 Lewis was in New York City conferring with coal operators on a renewal of the United Mine Workers' contract. He asked the AFL committee to postpone further conversations on unity until he had finished his discussion with the operators. The AFL committee said "of course" it understood that he had a lot on his mind. It has not heard from Lewis since, except indirectly. He did say a short while later that it was impossible to reach any accord because the Federation was in the hands of a "small group of leaders, firmly intrenched and reactionary in their attitude on public questions, who are tolerant of many evil conditions existing in the AFL." He also remarked that, as far as he was concerned, it was going to be a fight to the finish.

In January 1939, before the American Youth Congress, in Washington, D. C., Lewis again had his big joke in regard to labor peace. He then proposed that conventions of both the AFL and the CIO gather in the capital's Constitution Hall (D.A.R property the use of which had been previously denied to Lewis for a Miners' meeting) and sit on opposite sides of the aisle (there is no center aisle in this auditorium). And when this non-existent seating arrangement had been accomplished, the AFL and CIO delegates were next to accept or reject, and at once, his "simple" formula under which all CIO unions were to be taken back into the AFL,

235

chartered with full prerogatives, leaving all "questions of detail" for "later consideration." Even without its elephantine humor, this proposal merely repeated in essence similar suggestions which Lewis had put forth from time to time and which were spurned by the Federation. In this instance, of course, the Lewis "plan" was slapstick, molded to serve propaganda purposes, not those of harmony in the labor movement. Two days before this utterance, the President had put him on the spot by assigning to him responsibility for the bogging down of AFL-CIO unity conferences; and Lewis had to reply to this charge, somehow, if only for the sake of public opinion. Yet his answer was couched more in the terms of an ultimatum, with opéra-bouffe overtones, than of willingness to compromise. It evaded the crux of the AFL-CIO controversy: the existence of unions from both sides competing against each other in the same work territory. Besides, Lewis was fully aware that both AFL and CIO affiliates are self-governing entities (outside of the federal local unions attached directly to the national headquarters) and that before the details of any fusion of forces could be finally approved, delegates would have to report back to the officers and rank and file of their own unions; that the blitzkrieg agreement he recommended, on the spot, within a few hours, was contrary to the constitutional precepts of both AFL and CIO.

Naturally, all this enraged the Executive Council,

the members of which on the whole are neither as vicious nor as reactionary as certain radicals make them out to be; they are at worst, with perhaps a single exception, sterile and inept and over-anxious to be accepted as "respectable." Yet the majority of this AFL Sanhedrin genuinely want AFL-CIO peace, out of a sense of self-preservation if not of social idealism.

They are disturbed over the anti-union legislation pending or already inscribed upon the statute-books of twenty-two states, sweeping eastward from Oregon to Pennsylvania, and southward to Alabama. They are convinced that the AFL-CIO scrap has gone too far. They blame Lewis, of course; but their own minds are troubled. Several of them protest almost too much about their "clear consciences" as if they remembered with a sense of guilt the ejection of the seven original CIO unions in flagrant violation of the AFL's constitutional fiat.

For the past two years Daniel Tobin—urged incessantly by the President to "do something about it"— has been releasing "united we stand, divided we fall" statements as rapidly as he can get them into print. His Teamsters, with their 400,000 members, control more votes than any other AFL affiliate, and would be immensely strengthened by labor unity, since they often depend upon the aid of other unions, such as the Longshoremen, in a strike situation. A loyal Democrat, a spellbinder in the tradition of Brann the Iconoclast and

Chautauqua inspirational lectures, Tobin has arrived at the stage where he is looking for new worlds to conquer. He can go no further in his able, if unduly autocratic, administration of the Teamsters, where his quiet effective campaign to clean out various locals infested by petty and large racketeers is drawing to a successful close. He has for years had his eye on the post of Secretary of Labor to round out his career, and his second choice is that of heading the AFL, a distinct possibility should William Green step down. Naturally, Tobin is not averse to directing a greater, combined labor movement, especially since, as he warned the 1939 AFL convention, "the tide has begun to turn against the trade union movement of our country" as the aftermath of the AFL-CIO breach. He has discovered, somewhat belatedly, and under the impact of the depression, that labor leadership today must meet challenges and face issues far more fundamental than merely taking care of the boys. Yet Tobin's imperialistic attempt to annex the few extra thousands of the Brewery Union's truck-drivers, whose absence would destroy ninety per cent of that organization's bargaining strength, has marked him down among many of the AFL rank and file as just another big-shot politician, rather than the labor statesman he has of late been trying to become, and may cause him to miss the boat of his ambition to lead the AFL.

In the belief that only a welded AFL-CIO can save

the labor movement from a serious setback, William Green, Matthew Woll, and the calm, sapient, square-shooting George Harrison of the Railway Clerks are today more eager for unity with the CIO than ever before. And more or less alarmed by current anti-union trends and quite as anxious as others for labor harmony are such steady, competent council members as Harry C. Bates of the Bricklayers, Edward J. Gainor of the Letter Carriers, Edward Flore of the Hotel and Restaurant Workers, and Felix Knight of the Railway Carmen. George Meany, the new hard-headed, intelligent, vigorous secretary-treasurer for the council, who is very much on the make, subscribes to the view that it will soon be a question either of "labor peace, or labor pieces." And even George E. Brown of the Stage Hands, T. A. Rickert of the United Garment Workers, and Joseph Weber of the Musicians, all three of whom are rarely vexed by problems extraneous to the regularity of their own incomes, are beginning to feel much the same way.

The stern, cynical, Gallic G. E. Bugniazet, secretary of the Electricians, is still positive that his union is entitled to hegemony over the CIO workers in industry's electrical zones, and will have to be cajoled into a truce. Yet neither he nor the puissant president of the Electricians, Daniel Tracy, is going to be too stubborn in this respect largely because Harry Van Arsdale, one of the brainiest and most influential younger men in the

AFL, and business agent for Local No. 3, with its 16,-500 members, has been calling loudly for peace. W. D. Mahon, of the Street Railwaymen, is still in a conciliatory mood, even though the competition of the CIO's Transport Workers has caused him many jurisdictional headaches. Only William Hutcheson, chieftain of the Carpenters, is still adamant in his antagonism toward the CIO, but even he realizes that he will have to string along with the pro-unity majority. His union, which has recklessly raided others in the building-trades group, is extremely unpopular; and should the Carpenters make good their threat to withdraw from the AFL the moment a treaty is signed with the CIO, they would find themselves isolated and weakened. They could not then obtain that "joint action" support, the co-operation with one another by all unions in the building trades, which is indispensable for success in strikes and employer negotiations.

In June 1940 the return to the AFL of the International Ladies' Garment Workers Union, which enjoys a higher rating in public opinion than any other labor organization in the United States, promptly quickened the drive toward labor peace. David Dubinsky, president of the ILGWU, and perhaps the most sapient, capable, and far-seeing labor leader produced in this country since the young Gompers, has been for two and one half years the pre-eminent proponent of AFL-CIO combination. He is a chunky, swart, barrel-chested man, with the high-strung nervous energy of a racehorse, but with the endurance of a Percheron, and with that burning intensity of gaze more usually associated with pictures of the minor prophets. Before rejoining the AFL, he and his union exacted pledges from William Green and others that the Federation would move quickly and drastically to stamp out racketeering from its ranks; that the Executive Council would relinquish its assumed and unwarranted power to suspend any AFL affiliate; that the per capita tax of a penny a month per member, used for fighting the CIO, be devoted instead to educational purposes, first of which would be to sell the idea of unionism, and what it means, to the forty per cent of American workers who, according to recent investigations, still do not favor it, or approve of it only vaguely and "in principle."

Of the CIO's eight top-ranking officers, Sidney Hillman in recent months has stepped out in front as the chief advocate of labor unity. He has stated, time and again, that it is quite as crucial for 1940 and beyond as was the formation of the first CIO in 1935. Four of his fellow vice-presidents—the blunt, shrewd, "ground-gripping," tenacious Emil Rieve of the Textile Workers; the stolid, slow, reliable R. J. Thomas of the Automobile Workers; the courageous, quick, imaginative S. J. Dalrymple of the Rubber Workers; and the clever, cautious Reid Robinson of the Smelters—lean toward the Hillman view. The Scotch-born, canny, burry-voiced, tough-minded Philip Murray, who in manner and appearance resembles Lewis Stone, the actor, and who is perhaps the most gifted triple-threat technician in the labor movement, as organizer, administrator, and negotiator, occupies a somewhat middle ground. On the one hand the need for comity as preached by Hillman attracts him very much; on the other hand his loyalty to Lewis has been so deeply ingrained over twenty years of intimate collaboration that Murray would make no move in the direction of labor accord unless and until his chief first uttered the word.

James Carey, the lanky, young, exuberant, energetic, panetella-sporting CIO secretary, whose relationship to Lewis is that of an adoring adjutant to his general, will do anything his principal commands. And the order of the day is still to "keep firing." Until some social inventor can devise a chairman of the board post that in an AFL-CIO amalgamation would endow Lewis with an importance at least equal to that of the presidency of the new organization, he isn't likely to budge from his "no peace at any price" position.

Indeed, his tenacity of purpose in this respect was not the least of the motivations behind his break with Roosevelt. The reasons for this rift are to be found less perhaps in the manual of Nicolò Machiavelli than in the precepts of Sigmund Freud, less in *Realpolitik* than in the CIO leader's personality, which, in turn, can hardly be understood until it is realized that there are three John L. Lewises, each covering a different stage in his theatric and turbulent career.

The first Lewis was the young buck miner, the Samson of Lucas, Iowa, where he was born in 1880, and where at the age of twelve he was already working in the pit eleven hours a day for $1.60, and where at sixteen he brained a vicious "killer" mule with a coal-car sprag. In his spare time, from his nineteenth year forward, he began to immerse himself in Homer, the Bible, and Shakespeare to make up for the education he very much had wanted but which his parents had been unable to afford. In tribute to his ornate, tub-thumping eloquence he was elected local delegate to the United Mine Workers' national convention in 1906; and from this springboard his oratory and talent for handling people enabled him to keep coming up. By 1911 he was singled out by Samuel Gompers as a person of extraordinary promise, and was named special Field and Legislative Representative for the AFL. He was assigned for five and a half years to some of the difficult organizing tasks the Federation faced, in Calumet copper mines, in Pittsburgh steel mills, in collieries in six different states; and he also conducted various lobbying missions in the capitals of Wisconsin and Illinois. His chief concern remained coal, however, and the people in its pits. It was in his blood; his forebears had been miners in their native Wales, and his own father, too, Thomas Lewis, had been a miner in Lucas and in other Iowa communities and had been blacklisted for being active in the Knights of Labor besides.

At night John L. Lewis pondered the problems of Black Gold, its prices, its cut-throat competition in bituminous, its monopoly character in anthracite, the annual yield of both, their wage-scales, their freighting costs, their distribution methods, until his vast knowledge of the industry so impressed John P. White, head of the United Mine Workers, that he appointed Lewis as chief statistician for the union in 1917.

Although a coming man in the labor movement, he was scarcely known outside its ranks. The usually accurate *New York Times* kept referring to him as James Lewis when, as spokesman for the United Mine Workers, he conferred with members of the special Coal Commission just as America was entering the first World War. Yet this occasion for his first "big-time" publicity was far more significant, in the light of his later beliefs and behavior, than getting the wrong surname in press reports. Bluntly he told the Commission that the United Mine Workers would never tolerate government intervention in the coal industry, that questions of pay-envelopes and production schedules could be best adjusted, on an exclusively voluntary basis, between managements and the union, and that "arbitrary price and wage fixing" by any government agency was strictly taboo. He was to remain a disciple of Gompersism, of labor's *laissez-faire*, for many years to come.

Meantime he kept moving steadily up. In 1918 John P. White, president of the United Mine Workers, resigned to serve on the War Labor Board, and Frank J. Hayes replaced him as head of the union, while Lewis was chosen as vice-president. But Hayes, kindly, lovable, was a victim of dipsomania and was too drunk six days out of seven to attend to his duties. Hence Lewis, as second in command, took over the seals and functions of the Hayes office, guiding the United Mine Workers through the war, seeing to it that the terms of the Lever Act, under which the union agreed not to strike for the duration, were scrupulously observed.

But when, after the Armistice, living costs rocketed some 30 per cent, Lewis supported the demand of the rank-and-file coal miners for a 60 per cent increase in wages, a six-hour day, a five-day week. Coal operators, who by the hundred had become millionaires as a result of war-boom profits, scoffed at this "socialistic" request by workers whose prevailing rate of $5.00 a day enabled them, in terms of real wages, to buy $3.50 worth of goods and services. Government officials pointed out that while the Fuel Administration had been disbanded, the Lever Act forbidding strikes was still on the books, and technically in effect, since no peace treaty had yet been signed with the Central

Powers. From his sick-bed President Wilson denounced the idea of a strike as "unlawful and unjustifiable." And Lewis in the first of his dramatic and vitriolic exchanges with holders of high public office reminded Wilson by wire that the "Hindenburg line has been in Germany for a year," and from this fact alone it was safe to deduce that the war was over. Whipped to a new frenzy of egomania, Wilson took the Lewis statement as a personal affront, and declared that all the forces of the federal government would be used to prevent a strike, at a time when domestic and European coal-bins were empty. "President Wilson's attitude," thundered Lewis on October 30, 1919, "is but the climax in a series of attempted usurpations of executive power." And despite a federal injunction against the strike, he called it, assuring the 411,000 workers who walked out that it was a crime and a disgrace that "Today when the coal miners of this country in a justified attempt to improve their conditions, undertake a wage move, we find our efforts strangled by the President of the United States." And over and against the government's conversion of its powers into a bludgeon for the operators, Lewis finally succeeded in winning a wage increase of 27 per cent, or $200,000,000 a year, although technically the strike was lost.

In 1920 Lewis was made officially head of the United Mine Workers. He was forty years old, the youngest leader of an important union in the United States. In the first flush of this victory, and against the advice of his wife, the former Myta Edith Bell, a Lucas school-teacher who has done much to bevel the rougher edges of his diction and culture, he ran against Gompers for the presidency of the AFL, and was defeated by a 25,000 to 12,000 vote in 1921. And this two-to-one plurality was rolled up against him largely by the maneuverings of Matthew Woll, who, as Gompers's own emissary and crown prince, then exerted tremendous political influence within the AFL. In Woll's opinion the Lewis candidacy was not only a form of *lèse-majesté* against the Grand Old Man, but was also a threat to Woll's own ascendancy in the near future. Hence when Gompers died in 1924 and the scramble for the succession began, Lewis and Woll were antagonists fencing with unsheathed foils. But Lewis, who had displayed too open a contempt for too many of his AFL associates, and who had indulged in his favorite pastime of name-calling at their expense, was too unpopular, feared though respected, to be again considered as the man to wear the Gompers mantle. At the same time, he wanted to even scores with Woll, and to be Warwick if he couldn't be king. He therefore swapped and traded votes with other AFL sagamores, notably his bosom friend Big Bill Hutcheson, to lift William Green, the urbane, conscientious secretary of the United Mine Workers, into the presidency of the Federation.

In that same year, when liberal unionists were rallying to the support of the La-Follette-Wheeler Progressive Party ticket, Lewis—an ardent Republican—plumped for Coolidge, from whose hands he later refused the post of Secretary of Labor.

Meantime the coal industry—over-expanded during the first World War—was going into the doldrums, retreating before the competition of other fuels, notably oil. Once more Lewis pinned his faith to the doctrine of the survival of the fittest, pinning coal unionism to earth in the process. He signed with a dominant group of operators a new and special kind of agreement which was going to accomplish, he thought, three wonderful things. It was going to recognize the United Mine Workers as exclusive bargaining agents in the eastern and central coal areas. It was going to force the uneconomic mines, about twenty per cent of the total, to close down. And this in itself was to drive about 190,-000 pit-workers into other occupations, relieving the surplus of labor in coal. But this contract was merely a decoy; the operators chiseled on it, ignored it, bilking Lewis. The Mellon Pittsburgh Coal Company only led the parade when, with the ink on this new pact hardly dry, it shut down fifty-four union mines, and bought 125,000 acres of coal land in the South, hiring only non-union workers.

The result of all this thimblerigging was chaos in coal prices, drastic wage reductions, a growing rumble of revolt against the Lewis leadership. He was in the news less and less as the decade careened toward Black October 1929. The union was riven by internal dissensions led by Communist, Ku-Kluxer, and rank-and-file insurgents. And from 1930 forward, as the depression deepened, coal—for years a sick industry—seemed at last on the verge of dying. Mines were closed by the dozen each week, throwing thousands of workers out of their jobs. Many of them began to turn in their union cards, assailing the Lewis stewardship of their union, muttering against his thousand-dollar-a-month salary, his Cadillac, his chauffeur. Coal operators who were still doing business decided that the time was ripe to deliver the union a knock-out blow and gave preference to non-members for the remaining work. By 1932 the United Mine Workers had dwindled from a post-war high of 450,000 adherents to a new low of less than 90,000; although Lewis, to save face and preserve some voting strength at AFL conventions—paid a per capita tax on 150,000. After twelve years of leadership, he was slipping, putting down rebellions with an iron hand, but riding the whirlwind and unsure of his future. The general public heard of him only as labor's chief advocate of Herbert Hoover's re-election.

Like the bell that saves a groggy fighter, Roosevelt's election not only gave Lewis a breathing-spell, but enabled him to stage a strong come-back, to begin the

249

second part of his career. Early in 1933 Lewis was asked to Washington by Raymond Moley and sounded out for his ideas on what should be done for doctoring coal. And Lewis—chastened by his bitter experience with the laissez-faire agreements of the twenties—proposed to Moley a rough draft of what was to become the Davis-Kelly bill for stabilizing the coal industry. It contained, this draft, the nucleus of the entire NRA set-up, its fair-competition codes, its suspension of the anti-trust laws, its Section 7a promising to labor the right to bargain collectively through unions of its choosing. It was Lewis, along with his able, scholarly economic adviser, W. Jett Lauck, who helped to invent the essentials of the Blue Eagle recovery program.

And under Section 7a, amid a revival of the coal industry, Lewis saw his chance to recoup. He borrowed money for automobiles, even for gasoline, and sent hundreds of organizers who were willing to wait for their salaries speeding like motorized army units into the twenty-six coal states. "The President wants you to join," they chanted, "F. D. R. and John L. are buddies," they cried; "the government's on our side now," they assured knots of eager men clustering around them in mine after mine.

Within eleven months the United Mine Workers was bigger than ever before, with an enrollment crowding 500,000. And as the labor movement, under the New Deal's blessing, was revitalized, Lewis seemed to develop with it, to grow in stature with its every forward stride. He had arrived at the conviction that voluntarism, and all it implied, was completely unsuited for the motile, complex, interdependent society of America in the 1930's; that the strength of the labor movement thenceforth would depend as much on political as on economic action; that some degree of national planning was the way out not only for unionism but also for the rest of the United States.

From the moment the CIO was formed, Lewis loomed up as the second-best news source in the country. He was perpetually quoted, lionized, photographed, interviewed. He became the hero of two palpitant biographies. During 1936–7 he was one of the most vilified, glorified, feared, and loved men in the nation. He was also one of the busiest. He was busy with sit-downs, with negotiations, with lobbying for New Deal measures, with lauding Roosevelt as the champion of the common man.

In June 1937, however, during the Little Steel strike, first major CIO set-back, Roosevelt and Lewis began to pull in opposite directions. The President made his "a plague o' both your houses" remark and Lewis retorted that it "ill behooves one who has supped at labor's table" to remain aloof and impartial in a contest between labor and its adversaries.[1] Lewis's statement

[1] Privately, to newsmen, Lewis asked: "Which house, Hearst or du Pont?"

was a thinly veiled reference to CIO contributions to the Democratic Party's campaign chest into which the United Mine Workers alone had poured more than $665,000. And this episode also marked the emergence of the third Lewis, the crusading and confident commander-in-chief of a CIO that not only was bringing unionism to a thousand places where it had been merely a remote hope before, but was also to become, in Lewis's vision, the spearhead for a new economic emancipation that would go beyond the confines of an old-fashioned wages-and-hours labor movement.

"One of the great principles for which labor in America must stand in the future," he told delegates to the CIO convention in Atlantic City in October 1937, "is the right of every man and woman to have a job, to earn their living if they are willing to work. A citizen of the United States of America has a right to live. He has a right to work. We have heard much about the right to work. Well, let our people work. They have a right to a job. If the corporations which control American industry in their management of industry's affairs fail to provide them with that job, then there must be power somewhere in this land of ours that will go over and above and beyond those corporations with all their influence . . . and provide a job, and insure the right to live for that American.

"As long as the Congress of the United States," he continued, "and the Administration in power dodge that fundamental proposition, just so long will America be in economic turmoil.

"There is work for our movement," he went on, "and . . . there is support for it . . . the support of countless numbers of Americans who for decades . . . have been denied their rights, their privileges and participations . . . unable to live decently . . . unable to give proper medical attention or proper education to their children, because those who have been the masters of this country in the realm of finance and industry and corporate powers have not given them sufficient consideration.

"Do you know," he queried, "that because a man is underpaid his child has more chance of dying than that of a man who gets a reasonable wage? Do you know that the sharecroppers of the South who live on their $170 or $180 a year are neither economic, social or political assets because they get $170 or $180 a year? . . . Yet they are human beings and they are citizens. It is for the labor movement to demand a participation by these people in the bounties and blessings, material and otherwise, in our country. . . . It is for labor here to take up the task of representing these Americans, because these Americans for long, like Rachel in the wilderness, have been lamenting and wailing, with no attention paid by those who in the smug security of their own good fortune say, 'the poor were always with us—they will always be.' "

253

During the first two phases of his career, Lewis's chief asset as a labor leader has been his ability to identify himself with the hopes, the strivings, the fears of his followers—first in his own United Mine Workers, and latterly in the CIO. He has been conscious of his position as a symbol, as voice for millions who get the wages of America's work. "I am content to serve my people," he has told them, time and again. "But remember, I am only as strong as you make me." But this asset, this sense of complete identification with those whom he would lead, is a double-edged sword. Almost from the time the CIO became a permanent body, it has seemingly turned against him, turned into his chief liability, as a subtle change in emphasis has appeared to have swept over him in his relationship to his adherents.

When at the United Mine Workers' fiftieth convention in Columbus, early in 1940, he predicted of Roosevelt that "should the Democratic National Committee be coerced or dragooned into renominating him, I am convinced . . . his candidacy would result in ignominious defeat," Lewis was in effect repudiated, gently but firmly, by the very unionists whom he had guided for twenty years. In resolution after resolution delegates extolled Roosevelt and Lewis in phrases of equal enthusiasm, and it was only after herculean efforts in committee that a third-term endorsement for Roosevelt was staved off.

Never before had Lewis been so far removed from the wish and will of his "own people"; never before had he been so cut off from the roots of his strength; never before had he allowed his personal pique and preferences to carry him into the furious and blind lashings-out of frustration.

No novice in national politics, Lewis knew, as few men knew, the debt of labor in general and the CIO in particular to Roosevelt and the New Deal, which, for all its drawbacks, remained the only political entity on the horizon that for 1940 at least would be willing to assist unionism rather than retard it. He had been, of course, exasperated by various New Dealers, and disappointed by them. From late 1938 to the start of 1940 they had been redoubling their efforts to persuade him to agree to AFL-CIO accord. A vast variety of White House emissaries, Cabinet members, Senators, Congressmen, Labor and Commerce and Justice Department officials, and others with and without portfolio kept streaming into Lewis's office, even calling at his home. They argued for labor unity. They pled. They threatened. They invoked sweet reasonableness. The very intensity of this pressure began to fray his nerves.

At the same time, when, in reprisal for what they felt was his obduracy, they rebuffed him on patronage, or failed to include him in invitations to White House and other social functions, he reacted as if it were not just

255

John L. Lewis who was being ignored, but as if all labor was being insulted in his name—a very spectacular insult that had to be resented in a very spectacular way.

It was in line with this attitude that Lewis, who visited the White House three times in as many weeks before setting forth to make his Columbus prophecy, spurned Roosevelt's overtures for a truce between them. Yet had Lewis been willing to yield somewhat and bide his time and co-operate, he could have obtained anything within reason; for even insiders had overestimated his ability to "deliver" the votes of his followers. In any case, he could have helped write the labor planks in the Democratic platform. He might have secured a change in the Secretaryship of Labor, a desire close to his heart. But he wanted New Dealers to stop needling him on AFL-CIO unity, and he was so adamant on no compromise with William Green that the President finally balked, getting his Dutch up against Lewis's iron whim. It was a clash of wills between two strong-minded personalities, with the result that Lewis broke with Roosevelt because he couldn't bend him, at least not far enough, in a contest where the stakes spelled power.

And this tendency is a tragic thing for American labor. For Lewis, with all his faults, is a man of first-rate quality, even of genius perhaps, and to measure him you need callipers of more than ordinary size. He is bold. He is brilliant. He has on the whole displayed a rare capacity for growing in stature with each new responsibility. His moral life is impeccable. But—and it's a big "but"—he seduces the virgins of acclaim. He cohabits with the sluts and sirens of power. He has surrounded himself with Stalinist sycophants and palace janizaries who assure him that, as a man of destiny, he can do no wrong; or at least for so long as he allows them to try to lead him around by the nose. And in his genuine desire for labor to have a more effective voice in the conduct of industry and government, he has of late too often tended to confuse labor's causes with his own choices; and for so long as this turn of mind prevails it will remain the primary obstacle to AFL-CIO accord. Under such circumstances, for Lewis to relinquish his present top-spot post in the CIO, to become even the concert master of a symphony orchestra after he has conducted one of his own, would be a sacrifice of which he may some day be capable, but which at present he would spurn.

There are in all this, of course, two auxiliary points. The first is that the Stalinists, who for their own reasons are seeking to prevent labor peace, are still so firmly entrenched in the CIO that they could wreck a substantial part of it if Lewis should suddenly acquire a more pacific mood. The second point is embedded in what, for lack of a better term, might be called the biology of social organisms. The CIO is composed primarily of

257

younger men. They have been in the main recruited from those mass-production spheres where you're all washed up at forty. They have not only youth, but its impatience, its energy, its desire for action. Most of them have reached their maturity since the crash of Black October 1929. They have been subjected to all the blind alleys, the disillusionments that marked the dark dread decade of the 1930's. They want to "do something about it," to change a status quo which has so far refused to give most of them anything resembling a decent break. They think "differently" from perhaps the majority of AFL members, who have known more comfortable periods and are relatively somewhat more resigned to waiting for their return. The CIO rank and file, or many of them, tend to feel also that the AFL let them down during NRA days, and before. They regard most of the AFL leaders as mossbacks, or at the least as behind the times. They believe also that the Executive Council has tolerated racketeers within the AFL in a cynical mood of "Live and let live," and point to New York City and Chicago scandals in the building-maintenance and trucking unions for proof. And this is important, for the CIO unionist is very proud of the clean character of his organization.

On the AFL side similar sentiments prevail, if in reverse. Many AFL old-timers look upon the CIO as wet behind the ears, as being more of a mob than a movement. And on the AFL side, too, there is fondness for personal power. William Green would be extremely reluctant to abandon his present prominence, which he has worked hard and diligently to achieve. He is seven years older than Lewis, and was also a miner; the indelible blue spots in the skin of his round face are mementos of the days when, starting at sixteen, he dug coal at a colliery in Coshocton, Ohio, his birthplace. Like Lewis, Green is also of Welsh descent from a mining family. And like Lewis again, Green, because of his family's indigence, was unable to acquire the formal education he sought; and he was profoundly disappointed that he could not prepare himself for the Baptist ministry.

He was a sober, plodding, serious youth, an ardent "dry" who also eschewed tobacco and who taught Sunday school. He had early joined the United Mine Workers local in Coshocton; and by taking on the clerical and corresponding routines of the union in his neat precise fashion he was chosen its sub-district president in 1900. And six years later, as a reward for his "Steady does it" conduct of the union's affairs in the Coshocton area, he was elected president of the entire Ohio state district of the United Mine Workers. Popular with the rank and file, who respected his "respectability," he was with their support elected to the state Senate on the Democratic ticket in 1913. Despite the efforts of various Left-wing biographers to obscure and minimize Green's legislative accomplishments,

259

they were both considerable and valuable. He drafted and lobbied through bills which shortened the work week for women in industry, installed a pioneering system of workmen's compensation insurance, abolished the "post-screening" method of payment by which operators cheated miners on the amount of coal they had dug.

His success in these and similar undertakings landed him a promotion within his union to the post of secretary-treasurer; and a few months later, in 1914, he was named eighth vice-president of the AFL to represent the United Mine Workers on the Executive Council. Then, as later, he was distinguished by the same eagerness to see all sides of a question that has made him at once the AFL's chief diplomat and its chief acrobat, swinging from trapeze to trapeze in ideational spaces. He wants balm in labor's Gilead; and he has been pulled first in one direction and then in another by less pacific and less palliative personalities. He relishes his job despite its headaches, however, and even despite its necessity for fence-straddlings. By nature as conventional in thought as in his apparel, which is that of the conservative banker, he accepted the Gompers decalogue with no more questionings than he had given to the religion of his earliest years. He is the most intensively "middle-class-minded" man prominent in the labor movement, an Elk, an Odd Fellow, a born mixer, the epitome of the mores and conditioning of a Midwestern small town.

He is one of the nation's most tireless public speakers, before audiences ranging from Rotarians to university forums on "capital-labor" questions; and in this his presidency of the AFL affords him all the opportunities for that ego-expansion he temperamentally needs. In his first few years of office he was adept in the lilting platitude.

"I know as I speak to you this morning," he told a special organizers' conference in 1938, "that our thoughts instinctively turn to the greatness of our country and to our homes and while all of us come from different communities and sections which we call our homes, in a large sense this great America is our home and we love America because it is our home, and we are thinking about its greatness, its resources, the common heritage of liberty and democracy that has been conferred upon us, the breadth and length of our land, the greatest nation in all the world and we are happy to live here in America and call America our home. We want to make America what it ought to be, a land of happy homes where liberty, in its fullest sense, is enjoyed by all classes and groups of people; where he who lives in an exalted and influential position may enjoy all the rights to which he is entitled and where the humblest in all the land may walk in the orderly paths

261

of freedom and liberty and enjoy all the blessings that come to the rich and the mighty."

When Lewis to serve his own designs caused Green to be elevated to the presidency of the Federation, the latter—who is simple and unassuming—was only less startled than the rest of the labor movement. He pledged undying fealty to Lewis, for he was naturally grateful; he had with genuine modesty hardly aspired to such eminence and prestige. And Green did consult closely with Lewis for some years, heeding his advice, until with the decline of the United Mine Workers in the late twenties and first three years of the thirties, and with the corresponding ascent of the building-trades unions, Green began gradually switching his allegiance. To retain his titular powers he began more and more to favor the Hutcheson-Wharton-Tobin bloc which from 1928 forward controlled the AFL's inner circle. But this change of pace was not considered really important, or as anything out of the ordinary in organization politics. Certainly Lewis bore Green no grudge for keeping his fences in repair. Indeed, it was Lewis who renominated Green for the presidency at the 1935 AFL convention. It was only after the CIO was getting under way that Green was racked by conflicting loyalties between the United Mine Workers of his first phases as a labor leader and the Carpenters, Machinists and Teamsters of his later career.

And under the stress of combat with the CIO, Green

has tapped hitherto invisible resources of resolution and rhetoric. In fighting back at Lewis he has been stimulated into casting overboard the turgid beatitudes of his former days to declare in good muscular phrases: "I would not be fit to be the leader of five million workers if I did not possess a passion for [AFL-CIO] peace. . . . I am willing to go the limit, to let bygones be bygones, to bury the past, if we can only meet and settle our differences. . . ."

Naturally, in an AFL-CIO merger, neither Lewis nor Green could at first, anyway, head the new organization, if only because they have been for so long the embodiments of civil war. If, however, Green were sure that his own resignation would ensure labor unity, he would step down, regretfully, but with dignity, with all the proper Sidney Carton gestures, music offstage, and a slow curtain.

CHAPTER VIII

LABOR'S HOUR OF DESTINY

AMONG THE lesser lights of both the AFL and the CIO, notably the heads of union locals, the fear exists that amid the changes and shifts and rearrangements of any AFL-CIO crisis they might lose their jobs. And this fear is understandable. It is infinitely more difficult for an ex-union-leader to obtain a new position than for the professional man or executive. A union chieftain who has devoted twenty years to the vocation(s) he represents has a low market value elsewhere. He can know men's wear from buttonhole to opera cape, but that doesn't mean he could be very useful in bricklaying. Yet this apprehension, accounting for the passivity, the negative approval, with which many minor officials on both sides have greeted moves toward an AFL-CIO combination, overlooks the probability that a united labor movement, if it grew at all, would need more, and not fewer, men of executive capacity—as organizers, as administrators, as propagators of the faith.

From the standpoint of enlightened self-interest alone, considerations of personal security for union office-holders are now secondary to the exigent need for unity between the AFL and the CIO. In addition to the lessons of Oregon, with all their implications, the *Fortune,* Gallup, and other public-opinion polls during the past two years have recorded a rising tide of resentment against unions—a trend reflected in the growing demand for their "incorporation."

Of all the proposals to "regulate" unions, incorporation is perhaps the most unjust and absurd; and yet by sheer force of iteration on the part of anti-union employers, it has assumed—even in the minds of people who should know better—a certain metaphysical merit. The advocates of union incorporation claim that (1) it would end "graft and racketeering," (2) that unions should incorporate because business does, and (3) that the process would fix and promote responsibility.

In the first place graft and racketeering are no more endemic normally to unionism than cancer to the healthy individual. From the inside, it stems from certain corrupt and dishonest labor leaders who regard their unions in the same way that Richard Whitney, former president of the New York Stock Exchange, regarded funds entrusted to him—namely, as media for personal profit. Thus the notorious Robert Brindell in

265

the New York of twenty years ago became czar of the city's building-trades unions, kept the rank and file terrorized by means of his brass-knuckle brigade, and exacted tribute from contractors in the form of "strike insurance" lest Brindell suddenly discover infractions of union rules and call the men out. From the outside, racketeering occurs as in the case when Al Capone muscled in on the Chicago dry-cleaning industry and its unions, "shaking down" both owners and employees, under threat of taking them for a ride.

As a rule labor leaders who are identified with racketeering are merely a half or a third of the racket pervading the entire industry. Thus, Joseph "Socks" Lanza, business agent of the United Sea Food Workers Union played hand in glove with the wholesalers banded together into the Fish Credit Association to foster an absolute monopoly of the fresh-water fish business in New York City. The formula was simple. The retailer had either to pay the exorbitant price demanded by anyone of the twenty-five members of the Employers' Association, or the union, under Lanza's [1] orders, would refuse to handle the retailer's fish. Any dealer who refused to abide by this arrangement found that fish consigned to him from sources other than the Association were stolen, that trucks carrying them were wrecked, that stench bombs exploded under his counters. For

[1] Lanza was convicted and sent to prison for two years, and fined ten thousand dollars in 1935 for this activity.

five years Lanza enjoyed the protection of the municipal Democratic administration and allegedly divided
a part of his "take" with officials of Tammany Hall.

The whole question of racketeering in unions has
been blown up out of all proportion to the frequency
of its incidence. Otherwise, even granting the anti-
union bias of most newspaper publishers, the discovery
and exposure of a labor racketeer would not be played
up in such sensational fashion, with big headlines. In
this instance, too, it is the exceptional rather than the
usual that makes news.

Moreover, as the New York City Club's Subcommit-
tee on Labor Unions, composed primarily of employers,
has pointed out, incorporation "could place no serious
obstacle in the path of racketeering; on the contrary,
paper corporations and dummy officers might easily
lend themselves to the extension of racketeering activity, which "may be prosecuted under various federal
laws, among them the anti-racketeering statute of 1933,
the anti-trust laws, and indirectly the Federal Income
Tax Law."

But it is often maintained that to place capital and
labor on an "equal footing" incorporation of unions is
only the "fair thing to do." Yet this point of view neg-
lects the obvious fact that incorporation is a device
invoked by business firms to *limit* responsibility, not
to extend it. To be sure, in exchange for this right to
be born with the silver spoon of limited liability in its

mouth, the corporate enterprise accepts a certain degree of governmental regulation; but this is to protect stockholders, not outsiders. On the other hand, when incorporation is asked for unions by people outside its ranks, it is exclusively for the purpose of enabling unscrupulous employers to "plant" *agents provocateurs* in the union, to become its officers if possible, and then to engage in unauthorized and palpably illegal acts to make the union an easy mark for court action on breach of contract, or damage suits, to tie up its funds, to deplete its treasury by costly litigation, and by this means destroy it. At the moment it may be observed that the very employers who today are pressing for union incorporation may tomorrow be hoisted by their own petard. There are, after all, only two methods of incorporation: by states, or with the permission of the national government. In the former instance, incorporation might open up for unions all manner of wide powers they do not now possess or restrict powers now given to them; but in the second instance, the unions will demand *"tu quoque"* until all business is incorporated or perhaps licensed by the federal government, a prospect that would evoke meagre ecstasy among the directors of corporations which now enjoy all the latitude and immunities conferred by, say, a State of Delaware charter.

It should also be kept in mind that businessmen are not *required* to incorporate, and may conduct their operations as individuals, or as members of a partnership or of a voluntary association, as they please.

The third argument for union incorporation, that of "greater responsibility," is at once the most vociferous and fraudulent. It is asserted that once a union is incorporated, "wildcat" strikes would be forever banished, since the union would be liable for violation of agreement, and also for "injuries sustained" by the employer in the course of any strike by its members. But for two generations unions have been held responsible and suable by American courts, on these and similar grounds, notably in the Coronado Coal Company case, and in that of the Danbury Hatters, where union members were sued as individuals and forced to give up their homes and savings in order to pay the fines. In the *Society for the Advancement of Management Journal* some time ago this situation was clearly recognized: "With remedies of a civil and criminal nature," said that publication, "with union members subject to suit and to imprisonment, sometimes for acts such as picketing, which are not intrinsically criminal, how can it be seriously urged that there is no redress against unlawful labor activity? Is it not possible that those who advocate further regulation to add to these remedies are either unaware of the facts or are fundamentally hostile to unions and collective bargaining?"

The various expedients for the compulsory registration of unions, and the filing of their financial statements with some public authority, are cut from the same cloth as the demand for their incorporation. By far the majority of unions have their books regularly audited by certified public accountants and publish the figures in the official organ, bi-annually, as a rule. The distinction to be made in this respect is that between the possibility of occasional, twice-a-year public examination of their finances, and that of constant publicity given to them. In the latter circumstance, when the exact monetary strength of a union can be ascertained at any time by the employer, he has the upper hand in collective bargaining; for if he knows that the union's coffers are low and cannot support a strike, he can dictate the provisions of any agreement.

And it is germane to this entire question to realize that Thurman Arnold, U. S. Assistant Attorney General, in his drive to correct certain unfair practices of unions by applying the Sherman Anti-Trust Law, has premised this action upon the same fundamental fallacy advanced by those who clamor for union incorporation. Both assume that a commercial, industrial, or financial corporation and a labor union are analogous organizations. But the business corporation is fundamentally formed for profit. It is an organization of dollars. The union is a non-profit organization of human beings. The chief purpose of the corporation is to pay dividends; the chief purpose of the union is to promote and safeguard the interests of workers to the end that the creation of dividends will not too ruthlessly violate their rights as human beings who need and want food, clothing, and shelter on certain "health and decency" levels, and as Americans who are entitled to free speech. Actually, the union is far more analogous to the trade association, to the chamber of commerce, even to the fraternal order, than to the corporation—a rudimentary fact that has eluded Mr. Arnold and his associates in the Anti-Trust Division of the United States Department of Justice. Certainly there is not a scintilla of evidence in the American adventure to show any identity of structure and objectives between a corporation and a union, or that what may work well for one type of organization would do the same for the other.

And as part of his crusade to restore the still debatable and theoretical benefits of a completely "free competition" to the American economy, Mr. Arnold recently listed five of unionism's "unreasonable restraints" upon production and sale which he will not tolerate, and which he says are designed to:

1. Enforce systems of graft and extortion;

2. Enforce "illegally fixed prices";

3. Prevent the use of cheaper materials, improved equipment, or more efficient methods;

4. Compel the hiring of useless and unnecessary labor; and

5. Destroy an established and legitimate system of collective bargaining.

271

As a professor of law at Yale University, it would seem that Mr. Arnold might have discovered that ample legal machinery exists, in local, state, and federal laws, other than the Sherman Act, to prevent and to punish the first of these offenses without at the same time endangering the existence of all unionism, the major "good," with the minor "bad," which is precisely what his use of the Sherman Act in this regard is doing. When he approaches the second "abuse," that of illegally fixed prices, he has by implication lumped in the same category the stabilizing of an industry through uniform wage-and-hour agreements between a union and a group of manufacturers, and penalizing the public by monopolistic practices.

He has also brushed aside the plain intent of the Sherman Anti-Trust Law of 1892, which was devised to curb aggregations of capital, or what a man *has*, not combinations of labor, or what a man *is*. He has similarly ignored the unequivocal meaning of the Clayton Act of 1914 which declared that labor organizations cannot be "held or construed to be illegal combinations or conspiracies in restraint of trade, under the anti-trust laws," since "the labor of a human being is not a commodity or article of commerce."

It should be noted that Mr. Arnold wants to forbid all labor activity if directed to the objectives set forth in his five "thou shalt nots." But by failing to discriminate between the goals of a labor dispute and the methods of arriving at their adjustment, Mr. Arnold and his aids would subject the most conventional strikes and picketing to criminal prosecution under the anti-trust laws. He has drawn no genuine distinction between the abuses of unionism and their historical functioning, and this is a serious business indeed. Despite his honorable intentions, and he is a well-meaning if intensely muddled man, he is bogging himself down, and perhaps unionism with him, in the confusion between ends and means. He wants to obtain certain admirable goals; among them, for example, the breaking up of the building industry's log-jam that derives from high material costs and high labor costs, and from alleged conspiracies between employers and unions. The release of this industry from these and similar restraints would seem to be commendable; it should be done, it has to be done, soon or late. But there are other ways—the exploration of the annual-wage principle, for example, and many more; the ways essentially of the council table rather than those of the criminal statute. And in invoking the anti-trust laws against some unions which have indulged in practices which he considers to be contrary to the public welfare, he is opening the way for some less socially-minded successor to use the same instrument against *all* unions. He is thus throwing the baby out with the tub water, and at a time when the experience of other nations has taught us, as never before, that the means shape the

273

end; that their reciprocal relationship makes them one. In accord with his setting of a precedent whereby a good end is to be reached by a doubtful means, his three last prohibitions as to what labor unions can and cannot do are perhaps the most dangerous of the lot.

If a union, for example, may not draw upon its economic power to prevent the employer from using "cheaper materials," which in nine cases out of ten are sweat-shop materials, produced by non-union or convict labor under depressed or substandard conditions, then it has been deprived of a basic right. By the same token "more efficient methods" is most often a euphemism for the speed-up, the notching up of the "line" to drain the last ounce of energy from the worker; or of the "stretch-out," whereby a textile weaver, for example, has to tend 48 looms instead of 24. And who is to define "useless and unnecessary labor"? What is to stop an employer from driving his workers harder for a few extra hours a day, thus dispensing with the services of many formerly required, and then pointing to the new Arnoldian dictate that has neither sweetness nor light to justify this course? Finally, in trying to prohibit unions from "destroying any established and legitimate system of collective bargaining" Mr. Arnold has summarily annexed a province to which he and his department have no proper claim. If a bona-fide union pickets a plant to protest its dealings with a company union, for example, does this issue come under the

274

criminal statutes used by the Anti-Trust Division or under the provisions of the Wagner Act? Who is supposed to decide, these days, whether "legitimate" collective bargaining exists, Mr. Arnold or the National Labor Relations Board?

However, the malicious glee with which Mr. Arnold's onslaughts against unions have been greeted in certain sections of the press should be a warning to the AFL that toward the question of unfavorable public opinion it can no longer adhere to the outlook of the pot-bellied, gold-chain-dangling, back-slapping, moth-eaten labor lobbyist of a generation ago who thought that the AFL's public-relations problems could all be taken care of by giving an expensive cigar to a cheap politician. The generally anti-union attitudes of most newspapers and radio chains cause them to focus abundant attention upon the "bad" unions and their leaders, while the story of the "good" unions and their leaders rarely gets told. And AFL chieftains have tended too much to assume that the middle-class groups and the rest of the community were against them anyway, that it would be a waste of time to try to win, if not their sympathy, at least their neutrality; that unions must rely upon their own economic strength alone to gain their goals, and that the public must accept the outcome of any management-union controversy on a basis of "Lump it or like it." This is archaic, stupid doctrine, part of a past long dead. Today labor does not depend upon its own strength alone. It has been aided enormously by national and state legislation such as the Wagner Act, the Fair Labor Standards Act, the Norris-LaGuardia Anti-Injunction Act, the New York State Labor Relations Act, and many more. After all, government reflects to a greater or less extent what the "phantom public" believes, and follows the oscillations of public opinion with great care.

When a Willie Bioff, Hollywood head of the Stage Hands, a one-time pander, and today an alleged "shake-down" artist who cannot explain a rise in his income of $169,211 for the year 1937, is allowed to hold office in an AFL affiliate, he injures the prestige of the entire Federation just as a rotten apple can taint a barrelful of good ones. When George Scalise, former president of the Building Service Employees Union, who had served a prison term for compulsory prostitution, was hauled up on charges of extorting "strike protection" sums from sixty different hotel, restaurant, apartment-house, and office-building owners; when his twenty-seven-room home, his swanky cars and clothes were also publicized widely in the process, the impression was again conveyed that unions are a breeding-ground for racketeering. Neither his suspension by the union's Executive Board, nor his own resignation which followed next day, did much to dispel the odor of Scalise pollution.

Even conceding that the labor union as such is not

an adjunct of the state, and therefore lacks police and court powers, it remains spectacularly true that the AFL must clean its own house, and do it quickly. The toleration of the Bioffs and the Scalises and others like them and of what they signify has done the Federation an irreparable amount of damage. It presents an Achilles' heel as the target for the foes of any or all unionism. If the Executive Council, under the present AFL constitution, lacks the authority to eliminate extortionists and the like within the AFL, then the constitution should be amended, as in any democratic organization, to set up within the Federation a special and central tribunal as a character court, with perhaps regional subdivisions. It should examine and pass upon the qualifications and fitness of candidates for office in AFL unions, rejecting any whose backgrounds are suspect. It should be further empowered to receive and act upon complaints against the behavior of AFL union officials when put forward either by the rank and file or by employers and to expel those leaders who have betrayed their trust. And this would not be interference with the over-precious self-determination of AFL affiliates so much as it would be the common-sense expression of the doctrine that the good of the whole must transcend the preferences of some.

Naturally, in an atmosphere inimical to unionism, it is all too easy for the rank-and-file workers to give their loyalty even to a non-aromatic personality who, after

277

all, *appears* to be on their side. And this kind of allegiance, which is quite frequently enforced by the strong-arm squads of certain union chieftains, may be difficult to overcome. But its abolition is vital to the AFL's continued growth and effectiveness. It may be an arduous task to clean house, to get rid of the dark corners in cellar and attic, but in this undertaking the AFL Executive Council would not only obtain the gratitude of 99 and 44/100ths per cent of its membership, but it would also obtain a public support and sympathy that now is being alienated by the presence of an extremely small, but extremely vicious percentage of racketeers among its officials.

The CIO, of course, has an Achilles' heel all its own, its Stalinists. Their special menace to the CIO is not to be found in the popular conception of the man on the street that they want to "overthrow the government." It rather resides in the circumstance that, as servitors of the Comintern, their mission in the CIO is to gain control over unions in such key industries as shipping and communications, and to foment strikes, not to improve collective-bargaining conditions, but to hamper and obstruct the flow of war goods to the Allies, and thus to contribute their share toward Nazi-Communist collaboration throughout the world at the present time. That this policy is a constant threat to the regularity of wages for CIO workers, and to public approval for its program, would seem to be obvious even to John L. Lewis by now. The point to be kept uppermost in mind in this connection is that the Stalinists in the CIO are part of the foreign apparatus of the Russian government. Today they may be assisting Germany, but tomorrow—should the Soviet Union again change its international line—they may be assisting Japan, or even the British Empire. The peril of this kind of leadership in such CIO unions as the National Maritime Union, the Longshoremen and Warehousemen, the American Communications Association, and others therefore remains what it always has been: that the interests of the CIO rank and file are subordinated by the Stalinists to the interests of the Soviet Union.

In the re-allocations of personnel which would accompany any AFL-CIO fusion inheres a brilliant opportunity for the former to eject its handful of racketeers and for the latter to oust its fistful of Stalinists. It is, of course, fantastic to believe that men as gifted in intricate negotiations as Lewis and Green and other leaders on both sides cannot devise formulas by which, for example, the CIO Packing House Workers could be blended with the AFL Meat Cutters and Butcher Workers, or the AFL Boot and Shoe Workers with the CIO United Shoe Workers, and so on and so forth, up and down the entire list of organizations now competing for the same work territory. There are many precedents in labor history for these and other mergers. The United Textile Workers fused not two, but three separate autonomous unions: namely, the American Federation of Hosiery Workers, the Woolen and Worsted Federation, and the Dyers Federation, each of them retaining a considerable degree of control over its own affairs. A similar solution might logically be applied to the AFL's Street Railwaymen and the CIO's Transport Workers on a joint-board or joint-council arrangement.

A *quid pro quo* basis for such agreements unquestionably exists. In coal-mining, for example, the CIO's United Mine Workers with their 550,000 members is clearly the dominant union and should be permitted to absorb its AFL rival, the Progressive Miners, with their enrollment of 40,000. Similarly, if this principle of majority rule, which affords a certain safe if rough justice, is taken as a guide, the AFL's Brotherhood of Electrical Workers with its 210,000 members should be allowed to annex the CIO's Radio, Machine and Electrical Workers with their 100,000. There are, of course, many unions on both sides, such as the Federation's Actors and Artistes Association of America and the CIO's American Newspaper Guild, which are virtually *sui generis*. The former has no jurisdictional afflictions, at least externally, at least not with the CIO, while the latter is rivaled only by a few newspaper locals chartered by the AFL, especially in Boston. Both the Four A's and the Guild and other unions like them, on a jurisdictional plane all their own, could readily take their places as affiliates of a new combined body of labor to be called perhaps the American Federation of Crafts and Industries. Certainly in all essential respects, a synthesis of the AFL and the CIO is akin to merging two nation-wide chain-store organizations. Although difficult in terms of personal psychology, for it is undeniably a strain to deal with people who have made you the object of their best billingsgate, there are no other impedimenta to an AFL-CIO coalition which could not be removed in the exchanges of a conference where the will to unity, and the willingness to recognize that the essence of compromise is the making of concessions, actually prevailed.

The irreducible minimum of benefits that should flow from AFL-CIO unity already exist as a microcosm and example in Kenosha, Wisconsin, where both AFL and CIO unions refused to be stirred to the fratricidal frenzy marking the national feud. In 1936, in fact, when the AFL was busy getting ready to eject the CIO, the officers of local unions in Kenosha, representing both factions, were busy taking steps to immunize the local labor movement against the contagion of the impending national conflict. It was agreed, after several meetings, that a Kenosha local union whose national organization had joined the CIO would go along with its main body, but not much further. Neither the leaders nor the rank and file of any such local union would try to influence Kenosha unions whose national organizations remained within the AFL. Extremists who were noisy and partisan for either side were outvoted on this issue by a more level-headed majority. Hence the CIO locals in Kenosha never have been suspended by the AFL's Trades and Labor Council, the hub into which the city's union spokes are fitted. The CIO is still fully represented in Council deliberations, as during the past four years. And as a result of this whole program to avert the casualties of combat and to foster co-operation instead, the labor movement in Kenosha is strong, respected, firmly rooted, and the most progressive and civic-minded part of the community. Its political and economic powers are as unquestioned as the spirit of friendliness, even of neighborliness, that attends its rapport with other sections of the population.

Among the 8,500 industrial workers in Kenosha to-day, 94 per cent belong to either AFL or CIO unions. And more than 70 per cent of the city's public-service employees—teachers, policemen, letter-carriers, and others on government pay-rolls—are also union members. About 53 per cent of the service trades—retail clerks, barbers, beauticians, waiters, dry-cleaners—are organized and their unions are now rapidly growing.

With its 53,000 inhabitants, of course, Kenosha is a "typically American" industrial center of a kind placed in the 50,000 to 100,000 population range in business and government charts. Its biggest plant is the main branch of the Nash-Kelvinator Corporation, which employs about 3,500 industrial workers at the height of the automobile production season. Some 3,200 of them compose Local 72 of the United Automobile Workers, while the remaining 300 are distributed among locals of the International Association of Machinists; the International Brotherhood of Blacksmiths and Drop-Forgers; and the International Brotherhood of Teamsters, Chauffeurs, Stablemen and Helpers. The first is a component of the CIO; the latter three are AFL affiliates. No jurisdictional dispute has ever come up between them. Lacking the sophistication of their peers on the national scene, they are still "simple" enough to believe that the systole and diastole of unionism is unity, the standing together in a common cause. They therefore help each other. They exchange information. They pull in harness and work in harmony. Together they represent a hundred-per-cent unionization of the Nash-Kelvinator plant except for various supervisors and the bookkeepers, file clerks, typists, and others of the office force.

Virtually the same condition prevails in Kenosha's other main industries, such as the Simmons Company, manufacturers of beds, mattresses, and studio couches; an American Brass Company subsidiary; Cooper's, Inc., which turns out underwear, and other knit goods; and the Kenosha Full Fashioned Mills, makers of hosiery. In the Simmons factory, as at the American Brass Company's establishment, most of the workers belong to AFL federal labor locals, except for a few members of the Machinists and of the International Union of Metal Polishers, Buffers, Platers and Helpers, both Federation adjuncts. And at both Cooper's, Inc., and the Kenosha Full Fashioned Mills the majority of employees are represented by the CIO's Textile Workers' Union.

And this organization of Kenosha wage- and salary-earners into unions of their own choosing, and devoid of AFL-CIO animosity, has stabilized industrial relations to an exceptional extent. During the past four years precisely four strikes have occurred, three of them called by newly formed unions in the service trades, seeking to obtain "recognition." The other and more important strike was conducted by the United Automobile Workers at the Nash-Kelvinator plant, in October 1939, to secure a written contract instead of an oral understanding with the company. From labor's standpoint, all these strikes were notably successful, and a tribute to the solidarity of the city's unions, which, technically separated by the AFL-CIO schism, practically act as if they were all members of a single, well-disciplined organization. Moreover, the united labor movement in Kenosha has been able to sponsor and carry out a number of enterprises to promote the welfare of all the city's workers, and to do it with an efficacy and an *esprit de corps* impossible for a divided labor movement. Perhaps the most noteworthy of these so far is the publication of *The Kenosha Labor*. It is read in four out of five of the city's homes. It is edited by the brilliant labor publicist Paul Porter, who has made it into the finest "regional" weekly in the United States, dealing with domestic and foreign affairs with a rare amount of candor, insight, and alertness. Slim, scholarly, with a wry sense of humor, Porter belongs to that newer school of labor's liberals that has come to the fore during the last few years. They believe that an ounce of realistic accomplishment for labor is preferable to a pound of theoretical aptness. They roll up their sleeves for action in labor's daily struggles with the same gusto, but with far more sense, than their predecessors of the early thirties rolled up their high scores in rhetoric, and in almost that alone. During the past few years Porter has been among the chief exponents of AFL-CIO collaboration, and not only in Kenosha. He is the moving spirit behind labor's Committee of a Million which has already gathered from both AFL and CIO unionists more than 400,000 rank-and-file signatures to a strong, succinct demand for immediate labor peace.

Recently Porter pointed out the unique character of *The Kenosha Labor*, which, he said, "is managed by the Union Cooperative Publishing Company, owned by 34 local unions. The company, organized on the

285

Rochdale plan, is incorporated as a cooperative under the laws of Wisconsin, and the unions which own it vote at stockholders' meetings in proportion to their membership. This arrangement gives the AFL unions 56 per cent of the voting stock, CIO unions 43 per cent, and an independent union, the Policemen's Protective Association, 1 per cent. This ratio is an accurate reflection of the proportionate strength of the AFL, CIO and independent unions in the city. There has been no noticeable tendency," he continued, "of stockholder representatives in the publishing company to decide issues on the basis of AFL or CIO affiliations.

"The Union Cooperative Publishing Company," he added, "represents an investment by local unions of nearly $20,000 and does a yearly business of $35,000. The company also operates a well-equipped job-printing department and does the printing of a number of local business firms, as well as that of unions in Kenosha and nearby cities."

In addition to getting out their own splendid paper, the AFL and CIO in Kenosha have established a Workers Educational Council, enabling many unionists to tell what time it is by the hour- as well as by the minute-hand of the social clock. The Council arranges and conducts classes in American history, collective bargaining, labor economics, public speaking, and ancillary subjects. It maintains a free circulating library of some five hundred volumes, many of them dealing with current issues of special interest to labor. The Council also sponsors various public debates, forums, and lectures and recently arranged two state-wide conferences on how to improve methods of workers' education.

In Kenosha both the AFL and the CIO are active in the Kenosha Union Label League, which seeks to instruct and persuade unionists and the general public to look for union labels and to give preference to union-made goods in almost everything they buy. The League distributes free to more than ten thousand families an annual directory of products manufactured in union plants and shops. And in the event of competing AFL and CIO labels, as in men's clothing, with the AFL United Garment Workers rivaling the CIO's Amalgamated Clothing Workers, the Label League endorses the insignia of both.

Every year, moreover, the AFL and CIO unions jointly celebrate Labor Day. And to sidestep any show of favoritism, the speaker of the day is selected from outside the ranks of either the AFL or the CIO, while the All-Union Chorus and the Union Recreational Council, supported diligently by AFL and CIO alike, prepare the kind of program which is far more picturesque and meaningful to Americans than the yodeling Tyrolese festivals which lured tourists in such quantities before the outbreak of the second World War.

287

At the moment, in conjunction with the Cooperative Consumers of Kenosha, the local AFL and CIO unions are laying the groundwork for building a cooperative medical center to supply better medical care to workers and their families at lower costs. Finally, it is no coincidence that the hourly and weekly earnings of Kenosha workers were some three and one half per cent higher than in any comparable Wisconsin city throughout 1939.

If and when the United States should enter the present World War, both AFL and CIO are likely to be seriously damaged, if not entirely extinguished, under a dictatorship that might well prolong itself beyond merely "the duration."

The Industrial Mobilization Plan, the famous "M-Day" blueprint as prepared and revised over the past fifteen years by sixty army officers and sixty Mars-minded civilians, is predicated upon a labor movement that will let itself be pushed around, and with no back talk about it, either. Naturally, President Roosevelt's appointment of Sidney Hillman as labor co-ordinator on the Council of National Defense allowed many labor leaders to breathe more easily about M-Day implications. The selection of Hillman in itself indicated the administration's apparent refusal to be swept into a "labor reforms may be disregarded" course of action. Nevertheless, the very mention of M-Day is still a nightmare stimulus to high-ranking unionists in all camps, and especially to the labor movement's rank and file, for M-Day remains a sword of Damocles, as of Mars, over labor's head. The entire M-Day apparatus assumes a labor leadership deficient in brains and guts, and certain to cower—with the dithering docility of a Caspar Millquetoast—before the commands of its betters. The latter are to be the "patriotic business leaders" who are to run the key War Resources Administration and who with the President will fix prices, and wages, and otherwise "co-ordinate the functions" of the American economy in time of "major war."

By the terms of this arrangement, as soon as a state of war is found to exist, all labor is to be placed under the authority of a War Labor Administrator who is subordinate to the ranking members of the War Resources Administration. In the 1933 M-Day text, he was to be an "outstanding industrialist." In the current (October 1939) text he is to be only an "outstanding citizen," but his vast, his incredible powers remain as great as ever before. In this whole set-up the only representation given to labor is membership on an Advisory Council of ten, four of whom shall speak for industry, four for labor, and two for the general public. Yet this council, which in practical effect is a kind of company union with a fancy name, may meet only at the pleasure of the War Labor Administrator. And in conjunction with him it has to consider, more often merely to ratify his prior disposition of them, such problems as "measures to prevent grievances of employers and employees, whether actual or imaginary, from interfering with war production." The War Labor Administrator may also remove by decree such safeguards as the eight-hour day for women in industry, since the framers of M-Day plans believe that "many of these regulations and restrictions are expedient rather than necessary to the well-being of either the Nation or the workers."

The War Labor Administrator, in concert with the War Resources Administration, is empowered to control by edict all "standards of wages, hours of labor and working conditions" in the United States. He and his aides alone may determine whether or not "the effect of collective bargaining on industry's ability to meet the material requirements of the armed forces" will be to advance or deter the prosecution of the war. And if in his opinion collective bargaining hampers war efforts, he may without ceremony other than an executive memorandum abolish it. He may also, at will, modify the "statutory work day," and "suspend" all "restrictive regulations not having the force of law which unreasonably limit production."

Certainly an anti-union personnel in the War Labor Administration, under these blanket and Draconian war-time powers could destroy the National Labor

Relations Board, which ensures to the worker his right
to bargain collectively; the Walsh-Healey Administration, which guarantees union wage-scales on government projects; the Fair Labor Standards Act (Wages
and Hours) Administration, which puts a floor under
pay-rates and a ceiling over hours; the National Mediation Board, which settles industrial disputes on railroads. But all this merely suggests the extent of the
War Labor Administrator's omnipotence.

At his discretion he could also suspend the operation of state statutes relating to health hazards, accident-prevention, workmen's compensation, and the
like. Moreover, if in his opinion a strike, a boycott, or
picketing by a union for any purpose, even a demand
for a higher wage, should come under the category of
"restrictive" regulations, he may at once prevent the
union from striking, boycotting, picketing, or asking
for a raise in pay. Without resort to such prerogatives,
unionism may still march perhaps, but only with
muffled drums.

In testifying before the Senate Military Affairs Committee, Colonel Charles T. Harris, head of the War
Department's planning division, which is mainly responsible for M-Day proposals, cast some disturbing
straws into the wind.

He said that, whereas the War Department was naturally opposed to profiteering, "this is a profit system
in this country and the War Department feels that no

291

measure should be adopted which would in any way hamper or destroy the incentive to produce."

As a matter of fact, while M-Day authors virtually guarantee ample profits to industry, plus reasonable price protection, labor is given a work-starve-or-fight choice, but with no safeguards against the rising living costs which made the high wages of the last war a snare and a delusion. And for those who still cling to the myth that "labor also prospered" (remember "all those common, ordinary laborers buying silk shirts"?), it might be well to recall a few simple statistics. For the year 1917 the wage-rate was 112 and the cost of living 142.1; in 1918 the wage-rate was 130 and the cost of living 174.4, with food hitting 187 (basis: 1913 = 100). In short, labor on the average got exactly $1.30 in 1918 with which to buy $1.74 worth of rent, milk, and clothing.

There is another M-Day potentiality that the AFL and the CIO might profitably ponder. The Senate Committee which investigated the munitions traffic also explored thoroughly the War Department's conscription control plans and warned that "for all practical purposes, this country will have a draft of labor. The Government authorities could break any strike simply by drafting into the army the strike leaders and as many men as might be necessary."

And the minority members of the Senate Military Affairs Committee have also pointed out that the whole

M-Day set-up is a "bad bargain for unionism," which "takes the risk of death."

Yet even in these days of precarious peace both factions of American unionism are lighting the funeral pyres for their own immolation.

To be sure, both the AFL and the CIO agree on the need for the present national defense program, and in general endorse the view that the United States should extend all moral and material aid, "short of war," to any belligerent opposing Hitlerism. At the same time, however, the relentless pressure of many short-sighted employers to torpedo labor's New Deal advances may reverse laws now granting shorter hours and higher wages into laws to increase hours and to decrease wages, even if we should somehow evade participation in actual warfare. This, too, is the kind of attack against labor's hard-won standards that can be repulsed only by unleashing the full social power of a united labor movement.

Already there has been an incredible amount of ignorant, or merely malicious, editorializing to the effect that in our preparedness effort we "must not make the mistake of France," that a lesson should be drawn from the policy of the *Front Populaire* government under which pro-labor legislation and profit curbs are alleged to have impeded that unhappy nation's rearmament undertakings. But this line of argument overlooks the obvious, but vital, fact that the French and

293

American industrial systems (before Hitler's occupation of France) were hardly comparable in relative terms of plant capacity, ease of access to raw materials, water and electrical power, labor, cost, and fuel-saving devices, and the like. In factory mechanization alone, the ratio of American superiority has been around 3 to 1, and nearly twice that in motor vehicles; for in altogether too many sectors of Gallic industry a *modus operandi* of semi-handicraft and old-fashioned equipment continued to prevail even after war had been declared. Over the past twenty-five years, indeed, French industrialists, with a few exceptions, lagged behind Americans, Germans, and even the English in applying modern mass-production methods, in exploiting the potentialities of scientific management and new inventions. On the other hand, American technology has become the finest in the world. In the sphere of manufacturing productivity, for example, American assembly-lines, automatic cold strip steel rolling mills, and similar developments, enable the American worker to call upon such a vast quantity of "extraneous," or machine, energy that he could turn out three times as much as his French equivalent, over any given eight hours.[1] Despite all this, however, there are still the irresponsibles among our columnists, and editors and busi-

[1] Assuming, for the sake of comparison, that the theoretical national plant in each case would be operated at its full practical capacity.

nessmen who weep casuist or merely crocodile tears over America's "inability to produce."

Moreover, it should be recalled in this connection that during the year 1936-7, under the Blum government, the general rate of increase in production for French industries as a whole rose ten per cent above the preceding level. Primarily this gain was due to workers who had been refreshed and reinvigorated by having a little more leisure, and a few more francs to spend on food. The Daladier restoration of the longer hour and the shorter wage was less a measure of economic emergency than a political maneuver to defeat France's New Deal, the implications of which were alarming the two hundred families who collectively were his master's voice.

Yet the eagerness with which this wholly vicious and false analogy between French and American industrial establishments has been seized on by opponents of unionism, and its standards, is a warning that only the mad would fail to heed. For this velvetized variation of "guns instead of butter" is the kind of emotionalism that may stampede us, under the urgency of national defense, into imitating the most deplorable features of Nazidom, without duplicating its "efficiency."

A modern army, for example, requires seventy thousand separate and distinct items. It takes nearly eight behind-the-lines workers to keep a single combatant "effective"—fed, clothed, transported, and supplied in general. The staggering military might of the Nazis has been based in large part upon the constant, intimate integration of the factory with the fighting force. And it is a point too often neglected that, from 1936 forward, the most "pampered" section of the Third Reich's population, outside of the Nazi party's own bureaucracy, was less the soldiers than the workers in aircraft, artillery, munitions, and other principal war industries. To maintain their morale and to allay the discontents that flare up even with slave labor, they were among the best-nourished, best-clad, best-recreationed groups in all Germany. Certainly all this was not done out of any humanitarian motives, for Nazi labor cringes in fear of the knout, but merely to ensure peak production. It recognized the rudimentary fact that, in modern combat, material power is more important than man-power, that the people who turn out the seventy thousand items needed for today's army themselves compose a second army, the army of labor, quite as vital to success in warfare as the men on the battlefield.

In this country, too, it might therefore be realized that the worker who is badly nourished, or worried over his child's lack of meat and milk, or poisoned by the fatigue toxins of overstrain, or feeling that he isn't getting a square deal, cannot—save for short spurts—produce at top speed or with full efficiency.

On the basis of achieving maximum output alone, our

brass hats in military and industrial circles might remember that the average annual American wage of
$1,150, at current estimates, does not suffice to keep the
average family at a diet level adequate for continued
good health. The whole movement to "relax labor
laws," which is merely a euphemism for reducing wages
and increasing hours and for taking extra profits out
of labor's hide, is a primary menace not only to the
success of the American preparedness program but
also to the idea of making democracy work by working
through the ways of democracy.

To offset this and similar threats to democracy's survival in the United States, the membership and leaders
of the AFL and the CIO will be derelict in their duty
to themselves and to American society if they any
longer fail to press immediately, incessantly, and irre-
sistibly for labor unity. The present limited "truce"
for the duration of the national defense program, and
beyond perhaps, is surely not enough. The partial,
temporary suspension of hostilities is something far
different than the organic cooperation of an AFL and
a CIO integrated into a new single body. There is yet
time, there is yet a little while for them to conserve
their strength by thus increasing it. The extent to which
labor unity would contribute to national unity is, of
course, at once obvious and incalculable.

In this tragic and momentous hour in history, when
the clash of two worlds, the democratic and the totali-

tarian, transcends all else in mind and spirit, a free, strong, united labor movement must become democracy's first line of defense, if only because labor has long known that life without liberty is death without dying.

INDEX

A NOTE ON THE TYPE

The text of this book is set in Caledonia, a new Linotype face designed by W. A. Dwiggins. Caledonia belongs to the family of printing types called "modern face" by printers—a term used to mark the change in style of type-letters that occurred about 1800. Caledonia is in the general neighborhood of Scotch Modern in design, but is more freely drawn than that letter.

The book was composed, printed, and bound by H. Wolff, New York. The paper was made by S. D. Warren Company, Boston.